D0221056

Two Plays by Olga Mukhina

Tanya-Tanya and *YoU*

translated and edited by
John Freedman

 harwood academic publishers
Australia • Canada • China • France • Germany • India
Japan • Luxembourg • Malaysia • The Netherlands
Russia • Singapore • Switzerland

Copyright © 1998 OPA (Overseas Publishers Association) N.V. Published by license under the Harwood Academic Publishers imprint, part of The Gordon and Breach Publishing Group.

All rights reserved.

No part of this book may be reproduced or utilized in any form or by any means, electronic or mechanical, including photocopying and recording, or by any information storage or retrieval system, without permission in writing from the publisher. Printed in Singapore.

Applications to perform the plays should be addressed to the translator in care of Harwood Academic Publishers.

Amsteldijk 166
1st Floor
1079 LH Amsterdam
The Netherlands

British Library Cataloguing in Publication Data

Mukhina, Olga
   Two plays by Olga Mukhina. – (Russian theatre archive; vol. 18)
   1. Mukhina, Olga – Translations into English   2. Moscow
   (Russia) – Social life and customs – 20th century – Drama
   I. Title II. Freedman, John III. Tanya-Tanya IV. You
   891.7'2'5

   ISBN 90-5755-079-2

Cover illustration: A scene from *Tanya-Tanya* at the Vasilevsky Island Satire Theater, 1996. Photo: Olga Chumachenko.

CONTENTS

INTRODUCTION TO THE SERIES

The Russian Theatre Archive makes available in English the best avant-garde plays from the pre-Revolutionary period to the present day. It features monographs on major playwrights and theatre directors, introductions to previously unknown works, and studies of the main artistic groups and periods.

Plays are presented in performing edition translations, including (where appropriate) musical scores, and instructions for music and dance. Whenever possible the translated texts will be accompanied by videotapes of performances of plays in the original language.

LIST OF PLATES

(Pages 47–61)

1   Ksenia Kutepova as Tanya in the Fomenko Studio's production of *Tanya-Tanya*, Moscow, 1996.
2   Andrei Prikhodko as Okhlobystin in the Fomenko Studio's production of *Tanya-Tanya*, 1996.
3   The Kutepova twins, Ksenia and Polina, as Tanya and the Girl in the Fomenko Studio's *Tanya-Tanya*.
4   Polina Kutepova as the Girl in the Fomenko Studio's production of *Tanya-Tanya*, 1996.
5   Andrei Prikhodko as Okhlobystin in the Fomenko Studio's *Tanya-Tanya*.
6   Pyotr Fomenko and Ksenia Kutepova during rehearsals of *Tanya-Tanya*, 1996.
7   Valery Kukhareshin as Okhlobystin. Vasilevsky Island Satire Theater, St. Petersburg.
8   Valery Kukhareshin (Okhlobystin) and Darya Molkova (Zina) in *Tanya-Tanya* at the Vasilevsky Island Satire Theater.
9   A scene from *Tanya-Tanya* at the Vasilevsky Island Satire Theater, 1996.
10 Valery Dolinin (Ivanov) and Natalya Kutasova (Tanya) in the production of *Tanya-Tanya* by the Vasilevsky Island Satire Theater, St. Petersburg, 1996.
11 A scene from *Tanya-Tanya* at the Vasilevsky Island Satire Theater.
12 Viktor Shubin (the Worker) and Valery Kukhareshin (Okhlobystin) in *Tanya-Tanya* at the Vasilevsky Island Satire Theater.
13 Students of the Fomenko Studio, under the direction of Yevgeny Kamenkovich, staged the first public reading of *YoU* at the Lyubimovka festival in June 1997.
14 Polina Agureyeva as Pirogova in a student production of *YoU* at the Fomenko Studio, Moscow, 1997.
15 Ilya Lyubimov (Seva), Natalya Blagikh (sister) and Andrei Shchennikov (Dmitry) in *YoU*.
16 Ilya Lyubimov, as Seva, confronts Galina Kashkovskaya, as Yelizaveta Sergeyevna, Tomas Motskus as Stepan Ivanovich, and others in *YoU*. Fomenko Studio, 1997.

INTRODUCTION

I. The Environment

"Olga Mukhina," said playwright Mikhail Ugarov when announcing that Mukhina had won the Debut award for her play, *Tanya-Tanya*, in 1996, "is the Little Red Riding Hood of contemporary Russian drama. She had the nerve to go out there in the woods, not fearing the wolf."

Ugarov's joke, like most of what he writes, was on the mark. The first half of the 1990s was a difficult time for the vast majority of Russian playwrights. That is, writers themselves went on about their business. They wrote enormous numbers of plays, many of them quite good. The problem was in perceptions: An opinion achieved the status of a truth that no one was writing new plays, and/or that the few plays being written were either disgusting, silly, unstageable, or all three combined.

Those playwrights who succeeded in making the transition from the page to the stage were usually criticized and ridiculed far more than appreciated. A typical response to the production of a new play was to point to it as an example of why there was no such thing as contemporary Russian drama. That is a common lot for playwrights of all times and places, but let there be no doubt: The situation in Russia in the 1990s had become critical. That the attitude was unfair and mistaken was beside the point. The received opinion was broadcast as the wisdom of the day.

Enter Olga Mukhina who was still a teenager when the 1990s were ushered in. By the middle of the decade she had written a few plays that, for various reasons, had not attracted any particular attention. *Tanya-Tanya*, a dreamy, effervescent and sternly honest tale of love, changed that abruptly. Her fourth play, it was the first to lead her into the woods – or the jungle – of Moscow's theater world, and lead her back out again with a line of nearly tamed wolves trailing behind.

There was something almost magical about the response to *Tanya-Tanya* from the very beginning. Its public debut came in June 1995 at a playwriting seminar at Lyubimovka, formerly the suburban Moscow estate of Konstantin Stanislavsky. There it received a professional reading and was immediately singled out as a piece of extraordinary dramatic writing. Those who did not attend the seminar (I did not) began hearing rumors about an amazing new play within days of its being read. It was quickly accepted for publication in the prestigious journal *Dramaturg (Playwright)*,[1] and a production of the play by the Fomenko Studio opened at the end of January in 1996. In the ensuing months, productions followed at the Chamber Theater in Chelyabinsk and at the Vasilyevsky Island Satire Theater in St. Petersburg.

The speed with which *Tanya-Tanya* entered the mainstream was unheard-of for Russian theater at the time. People who had not praised a contemporary play since before the collapse of communism were charmed. Suddenly, one began noticing that critics, directors, actors and other professionals who belonged to different, often mutually exclusive and occasionally hostile cliques, were finding common ground in praising *Tanya-Tanya*.

Naturally, the acclaim was not unanimous; some were confused by what appeared to be Mukhina's drifting, amorphous, impressionistic and often unfinished dialogues and scenes. But for the first time in recent memory a consensus was forming that an impressive play by an undeniably talented writer had appeared.

Even if the legacy of *Tanya-Tanya* were to be little more than that – and it will be much more – its contribution to contemporary Russian drama would already be significant. This is the play that broke the vicious circle, that proved to large numbers of people with disparate backgrounds, styles and tastes that a contemporary play could look, sound and feel good when performed on the stage.

Despite the general lack of regard for new Russian plays in Russia, Europe has shown an abiding interest in what Russians are writing for the stage. Many playwrights, ignored at home, have kept starvation from the door by productions of their plays abroad, especially in Germany. But even here Mukhina outstripped her colleagues.

In the two years after *Tanya-Tanya* was produced at the Fomenko Studio, its popularity extended far beyond Russia's borders. As of this writing it had been translated into Bulgarian, Czech, French, German and, of course, English. Throughout 1997 Mukhina was visited by a stream of foreign theater dignitaries who had heard of her play and wanted to hear more. She was a frequent invitee at festivals where her play was either performed or presented in special readings (such as the Bund-Biennale festival of contemporary drama in Bad Godesberg, Germany, the Kontakt-'96 festival in Torun, Poland, the Avignon Festival and the Sibiu Festival in Bulgaria) or at premieres of productions (such

---

[1] *Dramaturg*, No. 5 (1995): 64–103.

as the Little Municipal Theater Beyond the Canal in Sofia, Bulgaria, or the Theater Na Zabradli in Prague, in the Czech Republic).

YoU made its first public appearance at a semi-acted reading at the Lyubimovka seminar in June 1997. It was an early version of a student production that opened at the Fomenko Studio in September. At Lyubimovka, the play was presented to a standing-room-only crowd of playwrights, critics, journalists and friends drawn by the hope that a replay of the *Tanya-Tanya* sensation might occur. If that was too big an expectation to be satisfied, the reading did evoke a lengthy and spirited discussion. The most prominent dissenter was playwright Mikhail Roshchin. He granted that "Mukhina is wonderful at creating atmosphere," but felt she was letting her buoyant style hover too close to self-parody. However, a steady stream of supporters took the floor, calling Mukhina a "playwright–poet," and pointing out similarities in her style to ballet and the sensibilities of the Russian Silver Age of the early 20th century. The playwright Alexei Kazantsev said of *YoU*, "This play is moving ahead of the theater. It will be very difficult to stage it."

Without seeking it or desiring it, the soft-spoken, unassuming Olga Mukhina found herself in the position of a standard-bearer for Russian drama at the end of the 20th century. That is what Ugarov really meant by calling her "Little Red Riding Hood." His reference to her youth was good-natured teasing; his admiration for her victory over critical inertia was entirely earnest.

II. The Playwright

In a blurb accompanying the publication of *Tanya-Tanya*, Olga Mukhina states she was born on Vesyolaya Street (that is, Joyous Street), and, indeed, one suspects she is right to have elevated that coincidence to the status of a biographical fact. Mukhina at first glance is an attractively absent-minded, lyrical, even mysterious young woman, although it does not take long to discern beneath the façade an impish sense of humor and a fierce independence. This is not merely a superficial description of the playwright's personality, it is an outline of the qualities which most prominently permeate the atmosphere of her plays.

Mukhina was born in Moscow December 1, 1970, to two geologists. (Her mother's name, significantly enough, is Tatyana, or Tanya for short.) In 1976 their jobs took them to the distant and frozen regions of Ukhta in the far north where Olga spent the next eleven years of her life. Upon returning to Moscow in the late 1980s, she began entertaining hopes of entering the screenwriting department of the cinema institute. Concurrently, she worked as a courier and secretary for the scientific journals *Quantum* and *Knowledge is Strength*.

According to Mukhina's own account, the trial scripts she submitted during the cinema institute's entrance exams over a period of years were repeatedly rejected as unsatisfactory and incomprehensible. Frustrated, she eventually tried her hand at writing a simple dramatic dialogue between a "he" and a "she" and found it "very easy" to do. When Mukhina completed her first play, *The Sorrowful Dances of Ksaveria Kalutsky*, she showed it to the playwright Yuliu Edlis at the Gorky Literary Institute who acknowledged her talent and admitted her to his class in 1991. (She was moved to the class of Viktor Rozov in 1993, but, at about that time, "just quit going" to the institute where she is, however, still officially registered. When asked one sunny spring day in Moscow in 1997, when the melting snow was running off roofs in streams, whether she ever expects to graduate, she smiled enigmatically and said, "I'll finish when it gets warmer.") Her subsequent plays have been *Alexander August* (1991, unfinished), *The Love of Karlovna* (1992), *Tanya-Tanya* (1994) and *YoU* (1996).

Since 1993 Mukhina has been employed as a scriptwriter and editor for a popular television show about pop music.

The first of Mukhina's plays to attract professional attention was *The Love of Karlovna*. It was given a shoestring, one-time-only production at a theater "laboratory" in Penza and Mukhina herself read it at a playwriting seminar in the town of Ruza. The Penza enactment was a turning point for the young author because previously she had been told regularly that her "untheatrical" plays could not be staged. But when she saw *The Love of Karlovna* acted out, she was encouraged to see it "turn out well." Despite an editorial preface noting that this "strange" play was supported by some and harshly rejected by others at the Ruza seminar, *The Love of Karlovna* was published in 1994 by the journal *Contemporary Dramaturgy*.[2] Its first-ever production opened at the Contemporary Play School in Moscow in March 1998.

The publication of *The Love of Karlovna* highlights some of the idiosyncrasies of Mukhina's style. All of her plays make use of stubbornly innovative punctuation and lettering. She freely omits commas and periods and increases emphasis both in the dialogue and author's directions by means of italics and phrases written in all capital letters. Furthermore, Mukhina intersperses amidst the text expressive photographs which are accompanied by captions consisting of imperfect quotes from her own play.

---

[2] *Sovremennaya dramaturgiya*, No. 1 (1994): 102–126.

All of this caused problems with the editors at *Contemporary Dramaturgy* who were intent on reigning in Mukhina's fanciful compositional style. Fight with them as she might, when the play was published, it was lacking all her pictures and captions, and the punctuation had either been "corrected" or left alone almost at random.

Users of the present volume will immediately note that Mukhina's photos for *Tanya-Tanya* and *YoU* likewise did not make the transition to the English versions (they have been included in some, but not all, of the translations into other languages). Lamentable as that is, there is a good reason. When composing the plays and collecting her photographs from books and magazines, Mukhina gave no thought to future publication, keeping no record of where she found the photos. That has made it impossible to acquire reprint permission, and so we were forced, with Mukhina's agreement, to publish without the photos.

As for the punctuation and lettering style, I followed Mukhina's lead slavishly. In the rare instances that I made changes, it was always done with the author's permission. Therefore, the unorthodox appearance of certain blocks of text in *Tanya-Tanya* and *YoU* is not due to typographical errors; it is a sign of the author's wish to cut through the conventions of writing and communicate nuances of emotional or psychological states directly to the reader.

III. The Plays

Tanya-Tanya is a mellifluous, buoyant embellishment of the eternal complications of loving and being in love. I purposefully avoid writing the simpler phrase, "of love," because Mukhina's characters are caught up in such constant inner motion, such agitation and such doubt, that the more common wording is too static to do those experiences justice. The play is written in a whisper, the kind two lovers share in intimate moments and the kind lonely, abandoned lovers are apt to utter to themselves in private moments of despair. Indeed, many of the exchanges between characters in *Tanya-Tanya* are probably simultaneous inner dialogues. This imparts to the play its velvety lyricism while Mukhina's withering honesty about the way people in love behave is what makes its characters so close and understandable to us.

To an extent, *Tanya-Tanya* is a literal expansion of Chekhov's famous declaration that he was filling *The Seagull* with "five poods of love."[3] Six of the seven characters are ensnared in what might be termed a Rubik's

---

[3] Letter of October 21, 1895 to Alexei Suvorin.

cube of love which, no matter how you turn it, cannot be resolved. The glorious absurdity of the interlacing relationships becomes apparent in even the simplest attempt to define them.

The contortions evolve at the suburban home of Vasily Okhlobystin, a hospitable man who is approaching that age when he suddenly realizes there is no turning back to youth. He is in love with Tanya, who, although angry at her husband for his not-so-innocent flirtations with a Girl also named Tanya, cannot and will not return Okhlobystin's affections. Tanya does, however, move into Okhlobystin's house along with his other house guest, the delightfully obtuse and ferociously independent Zina, long enough to get a perspective on her husband's behavior. Zina is in love with Okhlobystin, who sees in her little more than an outlet for his flirtatious energy. Ivanov's jealousy of his wife leads him to ignore the Girl, who suffers her rejection so deeply she is barely able to tolerate the devotion which the Boy heaps on her. He drowns his sorrows by courting the significantly older Zina, who, out of pity and understanding, encourages him more than Okhlobystin would have her do.

In the middle of this swarm of fluctuating affections, the comic figure of the Worker – not coincidentally named Uncle Vanya – appears to repair the damage done to Okhlobystin's house by the jealous Ivanov. Instead, the three men in competition for the attentions of the women, encouraged by a pleasant alcoholic buzz, turn on the poor Worker and he barely escapes in one piece.

All of this, including the final split-second of a hint of tragedy, is carried out in a champagne-induced haze of flirting, laughter, dancing and kissing. Early in Part Two the Girl hears some music and exclaims how beautiful it is. Says the Boy, intoxicated with love, "The air is ringing!" That can be said of the entire atmosphere of *Tanya-Tanya*. It rings with laughter, hope and music, and it rings with the transparent but insistent warning that behind the intense joys of life something potentially dark and hollow lurks. The joys in Mukhina's drama, as real and cheerful as they are, are not frivolous. They are poetic and they are earned. They are what some people have been able to muster or salvage in order to stave off loneliness and hopelessness.

The individuals of *Tanya-Tanya* are free, unique and autonomous. There is not a breath of the social in this play, and I suspect that is one of the reasons why it struck so many as such an innovative force. Russian art of all genres has traditionally been strong in finding and illuminating the links between the personal and the social. Even Chekhov's sarcastic doctors and philosophizing officers feel that strong urge to be a part of a national community. To be sure, Tanya, Okhlobystin and the rest are integral parts of their own social group, but those of their interests, needs and desires, which are examined by Mukhina, are strictly of a personal nature. When the Worker comes in from the outside and tells stories of people beyond the pale of the play, his topic is a farcical one of love and personal happiness. Similarly, the quotes from the poetry of Vladimir Mayakovsky – officially, anyway, the most public and socially committed poet of the Soviet era – present him in an unusual light. Here he is the poet wrapped up in his own personal tragedy, crude at times, sometimes lyrical, and thoroughly anti-social.

Another aspect which appears as a short flash in *Tanya-Tanya*, but recurs as one of the key elements in *YoU*, is Mukhina's patriotism, a patriotism that has nothing to do with politics. Mukhina's love for her hometown of Moscow is akin to Woody Allen's love for New York or Fellini's love for Rome. It is a deeply-felt affection for a city's personality, an atmosphere that permeates everything that happens or is said. Okhlobystin, whom Tanya quotes as once having said "I love Moscow and this wet snow," would have his life become "one funny little Sretenka Street," a reference to an atmospheric thoroughfare in central Moscow. Notably, both of Okhlobystin's utterances are made at moments when he is in the grips of love and longing. In Mukhina's dramatic world, that is a natural connection.

Tanya-Tanya is a tender, poetic play. That is in part due to Mukhina's choices of words. The dialogue in the fourth scene of Part One, for instance, revolves around the word and concept of "tenderness." Moreover, many of the stage directions are as excerpts from stream-of-consciousness poetry. One of them from the end of the play's first scene reads: "A vase falls from the table and breaks with an evening peal sadly squealing before falling from the table with a peal and the evening vase – violet and porcelain – breaks with a sad peal." Such rolling, impressionistic descriptions are there to evoke atmosphere and influence perceptions much more than to describe action. Furthermore, the people of the play are sensitive, intelligent and civilized, even when they are rude or crude. All are members of that nebulous category, the Russian intelligentsia, cultured people of learning, upbringing and conscience. They are more than a little eccentric, and their eccentricities make them all the more vulnerable and endearing.

Herein lies a genealogical connection with the characters of Chekhov, a writer who obviously holds Mukhina's fascination. Bits and pieces amputated from the Chekhov canon crop up frequently. And it is important to note that they are, indeed, fragments or debris. Mukhina sifts through Chekhov the way an archaeologist probes sand at a dig. What we get in *Tanya-Tanya* and *YoU* is something like the ruins of *Uncle Vanya* or *The Cherry Orchard* reconsidered and reconstructed. Mukhina's creation is whole and independent, but she drops signs here and there, letting us know Chekhov once passed this way.

That is evident in the Worker's name of Uncle Vanya. He has nothing to do with Chekhov's character and that is Mukhina's "point." She is out to conquer Chekhov, to overturn him. Chekhov's plays have had such a tight grip on Russian drama and theater at the end of the 20th century, newcomers have been unable to establish themselves in his shadow. Mukhina is out to use Chekhov in her battle "against" him. The strings which Okhlobystin notes are "humming in the air," in a short Part Two monologue, are a reversal of the famous eerie twang of the "broken string" in *The Cherry Orchard*. It is as if Mukhina took it upon herself to dispel that "mournful" sound which has become so closely associated, rightly or wrongly, with Chekhov's status as the bard of twilight Russia.

The notion of optimism is crucial to an understanding of the success and the accomplishment of *Tanya-Tanya*. The first half of the 1990s were not an easy time for Russians in any sphere, whether it was politics, economics or the social realm. As a result, the populace – including the theater-makers and theater-goers – was nervous and hypersensitive. *Tanya-Tanya* recovered for them the equilibrium of life's basic values and pursuits. One delightfully flippant exchange in the play's first scene, where an historical icon is toppled gaily, illustrates the point well:

OKHLOBYSTIN: Where do you live, Zina?
ZINA: Let's say – Lenin Street.
OKHLOBYSTIN: Maybe we could say something else?
ZINA: Maybe. Such as?
OKHLOBYSTIN: Let's say I'm going to kiss you.

The closest *Tanya-Tanya* comes to grappling with any of the social or historical problems of its time is to ignore them blithely. That was the charm that startled observers so when the play first appeared. Audiences will return to it repeatedly in the future because of its imagination, its sincerity and its uncanny ability to reveal the beauty in people drawing close to one another as well as in their drifting apart.

YoU, whose Russian title consists of the single letter ю ("yu") and is intended to resonate with the English word "you," contains the same excavated references to Chekhov's drama, as in cherries falling from trees; a character's call of "To Moscow!" evoking laughter; and a woman frittering away the minutes of everyone's life by incessantly serving them tea. As in *Tanya-Tanya*, the literary "quotes" are not genuflections, but rather Mukhina's declarations of independence. Beyond that, *YoU* is a broader and more ambitious work than *Tanya-Tanya*, and may even be something of Mukhina's own response to the isolationist quality of the earlier play.

In any case, *YoU* has the feel of confidence and the mark of daring. The dialogues, like casual human speech and thought, break up and veer off in unexpected directions even more than in *Tanya-Tanya*. The play's world is greatly expanded, containing representatives of at least three, maybe even four generations. The outside world is not only a part of the play's purview, several of the scenes actually seem to take place outdoors on Moscow's streets where automobiles race by monuments to great men, ensembles of Mexican street musicians play for passersby and lovers sit huddled on benches.

Some of the characters in *YoU* are largely of the same dreamy, reflective stock as their counterparts in *Tanya-Tanya*, and many are engaged in the same pursuit of romantic fulfillment. But a darker background crept into the more recent play. The joyous drinking in *Tanya-Tanya* now takes on connotations of an escape from despair. Seva, who watches his wife slip into an affair with a younger man, and Andrei, who feels an outcast in his own hometown, are prone to deep depression. Furthermore, the Moscow of this play (conceived and written while the war in Chechnya was still going on) is caught in the grips of an unidentified war that no one wants to acknowledge. War rages and life goes on. There are the occasional signs that cannot be overlooked, such as the sounds of shooting or a character being wounded, but the basic attitude to it all is summed up in a comment made by the unnamed Sister, Seva's wife. "When is this war going to end?" she asks. "This is really getting annoying!"

The elderly Stepan occasionally wants to listen to the news on his radio, but his wife Yelizaveta will have nothing of it. "This summer," she says, "we're living without calendars. We're going to focus ourselves on apples, cucumbers and blooming trees."

Appearing from time to time are a pair of old women in the manner of Shakespearean, soothsaying witches. They chant seeming nonsense, tease, mock, annoy and observe. No one understands them, nor does anyone like them much. But, like the war that seethes on abstractly, they will not go away.

Literally soaring above them all is a character we never see, Vitya the pilot. He strafes the town from time to time, although it is never entirely clear why; perhaps it is an activity of his participation in the war or perhaps he is merely showing off for his girlfriend, the impressionable Pirogova. This smudging of motives is typical of Mukhina. For while Vitya is one of the play's most constant symbols of the unseen war, he is also, at least for Pirogova, a romantic ideal. This deliberate confusion probably suggests something about the eternal seductiveness of war and warriors, just as it implies something about the enduring blindness and simplicity of lovers. After all, Pirogova eventually learns Vitya is married to a woman who is a "really great cook" and has eight children. But Mukhina never goes beyond suggestions. Any attempt to actually draw such parallels or discern such moralizing statements either among the characters or in the playwright's own attitudes is doomed to failure. Mukhina remains impressionistic to the end, often providing glimpses or tossing out hints, but never making pronouncements.

If *Tanya-Tanya* deliberately isolates people wrapped up in their own personal problems and desires at Okhlobystin's hermetic country home, *YoU* is an ongoing dialogue between the personal and the public. Neither is held up as either superior or inferior; they coexist naturally. One sympathizes with the righteous indignation of Sister or of her mother Yelizaveta when they get fed up with the war and want to ignore it and get on with the business of their lives. One also understands the frustration of Stepan who realizes that ignoring the war will not make it go away. Still, the most daring move he seems capable of making (while silently observing what seems to be the occasional flaring up of an old affair between his wife and their friend Barsukov) is to turn on his radio and listen to the news in defiance of his wife.

Mukhina's own sentiments are probably best reflected in the two obstinate old women who seem eternally to be hanging out in the corridor outside Yelizaveta and Stepan's apartment. Much of what they actually say is incomprehensible, perhaps like any true wisdom, but there is no mistaking what they are up to. They are irritants – incessantly after these sometimes vain and petty, but always vulnerable and attractive people to stop and take stock of themselves. The old hags' recipes for making meat pies, their incantations about the dead and their riddles about getting pregnant sound like nonsense. But it is the very enigma of their words which is intended to jar the other characters – and us – out of the rut of commonplace thoughts.

Mukhina, I think, would appreciate the popular American phrase from the Vietnam War era: "Make love, not war." To a large extent, that is what *YoU* is about. If the people of her play are guilty of criminal apathy in regards to the war they choose not to see, they are redeemed by their capacity for love. That is not a statement intended to evoke sensations of joy and happiness. As in *Tanya-Tanya*, affections, affairs and betrayals have nearly everyone hanging on tenterhooks. At least one, Seva, becomes suicidal and murderously aggressive as a result. There is a tangible sense of danger that shades almost all the relations among people in *YoU*.

And yet, even in that peril Mukhina finds room for redemption. In the finale, the youngest and most idealistic of the men in the play, Dmitry and Nikolai, suddenly postpone going off to war, even if it is for only a moment. Instead, they run after some girls they happen to see walking by on the street, threatening them gaily with kisses. The old women comment on that lighthearted development with their usual ambiguity – does that make the boys heroes? One old woman is not so sure, the other suspects it does. I think Mukhina, and we with her, are inclined to agree with the latter.

The notion of heroism is raised early in *YoU*, when one of the characters calls Dmitry, the young soldier returning from the war, a hero. But it is his optimism and his love of life which sets him apart, not his conduct on the battlefield. "Everything is so beautiful!" he tells Anya, perhaps his former high-school sweetheart. "You are beautiful. Moscow is beautiful."

It is hard to explain to those who have not experienced life in Moscow in the 1990s what an unusual, even revolutionary character Mukhina created in Dmitry. After seventy-odd years of Bolshevik heroes ready to die in a volley of bullets for the right to be called a communist, the idea of heroism of any kind seemed permanently compromised. Furthermore, the notion of patriotism – an ideological necessity under the Soviets and, most often, nationalistic jingoism among the patriots who followed them – was hardly in better shape.

Mukhina, ever the fearless Little Red Riding Hood, dove into the fray and recovered both concepts in their unsullied, original forms. Dmitry's heroism consists not only in his unabashed optimism, his flat refusal to be dirtied by cynicism, but also in his bright affection for his hometown – its tree-lined avenues, its laughing girls, its funny, rumbling trolleys. There is nothing exhortative about Dmitry, or about Mukhina's presentation of him. His naturalness and believability belong to her as well, and that is why both of them – the character and his creator – are so attractive and persuasive in their arguments. As is reflected in the following excerpt from the play's first scene, understatement is the key, no matter how lofty the topic:

DMITRY: I really love this city.
ANDREI: I love this city too.
DMITRY: I love my country.
ANYA: I love it too. So what of it?

Mukhina, however, went beyond the mere resurrection of some tainted concepts. She also attempted to redefine in an honest, but ultimately positive light, the shape of life in Moscow at the end of the 1990s. That is evident in her attack on the political apathy which affected not only her generation, but older ones as well. It is also evident in her almost cinematic (her old affinity coming to the fore) inclusion of Moscow street life within a medium, theater, that much prefers the limitations of an enclosed room and a couple of chairs.

Lillian Hellman, a suspect, yet oft-cited source, once sniffed that "Moscow was always an ugly city."[4] Mukhina, who knows the city far more intimately than the occasional visitor Hellman, sees something else. The "haphazard" sprawl that so irritated the churlish author of *The Little Foxes* is just what Mukhina recognizes as beauty. The clashes of Moscow – reflected in the first stage direction describing white Rolls-Royces streaking along the same road with crude, clattering flat-bed trucks – are the city's strength. Another image taken from the play's initial stage direction immediately signals Mukhina's dual attitude: "It smells of rain," she writes, but "a huge sun shines over the entire city." Moscow is diverse, changeable, unexpected, threatening and welcoming at every turn. It is a city that can crush those who aren't up to its challenges; it can be an almost fairy-tale wonderland for those who are. Indeed, Mukhina repeatedly uses the imagery of fairy tales or at least childlike impressions in the play. But most important, Moscow is a city with a long memory and a big soul.

Even those whose relationship to Moscow is more complex than Dmitry's cannot deny its charms. Andrei, the man of forty who feels Moscow does not love him, cannot help but say in jealous anguish, "HEY, MOSCOW – I wish I could scream in your face hanging on the step of a train leaving forever. I'll put on my white cape and get in my blue car and I'll drive your streets all night long throwing money at policemen on the way. Just to spite you! I'll ride you up one side and down the other. I'll hit all your romantic parks and all your Crimean Bridges. You'll come begging to me yet!"

Mukhina in *YoU* set out to create a modern iconography of Russia's central city. There is something in her effort that recalls the photography of Alexander Rodchenko in the 1920s or some of the films in the late '50s and early '60s.[5] I do not mean Mukhina used those works as a guide, but her love affair with the spirit of the city is a recurring one among Russian artists. She is the most recent playwright to make it a prominent element of her art. That she did so with such ease at a time when monotone negativity and cynicism came so naturally to so many of her contemporaries is another sign of her independence and originality.

---

[4] *An Unfinished Woman: A Memoir* (New York: Bantam, 1974), 149.
[5] Primarily I have in mind such films as Mikhail Kalatozov's *The Cranes Are Flying* (1957) and Georgy Daneliya's *I Stride About Moscow* (1964).

Alexei Kazantsev, twice Mukhina's age and, as the co-editor of *Dramaturg*, her publisher, has said that Olga Mukhina was one of his most significant personal revelations in the 1990s.[6] This kind of respect among peers, echoed in the comments of Mikhail Ugarov, is relatively rare. However, *Tanya-Tanya* and *YoU* are two plays that readily encourage such admiration.

It is a slippery business predicting the lasting power of contemporaries. But I feel safe suggesting that Olga Mukhina has already established herself as one of the boldest, most innovative voices among the current Russian playwrights.[7]

JOHN FREEDMAN
Moscow, 1998

---

[6] This was a comment made to me in May 1997.
[7] I would like to thank Theodore Shank for the comments he made after reading an early version of this collection.

TANYA-TANYA

CHARACTERS

TÁNYA
IVÁNOV
THE BOY
THE GIRL
VASÍLY (Vásya) OKHLOBÝSTIN
ZÍNA – *a woman whose youth was ruined by geometry*
A WORKER

PART ONE

Women Always Laugh and Dance

Okhlobystin has a large home in Bibirevo. There is a large garden around it with large apple trees and old benches that have sunk their roots deep into the ground. The weather is marvelous every day in the garden. Birds are always singing and in the pond there are many large perch. The house is filled with guests and women. The women are always laughing and dancing. Okhlobystin loves them with all his heart.

SCENE ONE

Ivanov

Okhlobystin's house. Gay, loud music plays. Zina and Okhlobystin dance and laugh. Ivanov and the Girl sit at a large table. They are silent.

OKHLOBYSTIN: Zina, what do you love?

ZINA: To dance until I drop!

OKHLOBYSTIN: Is that all?

ZINA: Nothing else interests me!

OKHLOBYSTIN: You have a great body!

ZINA: You're a smart-aleck!

OKHLOBYSTIN: I'm going to bite you!

ZINA: Ha-ha!

OKHLOBYSTIN: You don't believe me?

ZINA: (*Sits at the table*) My God, what is this? He's going to eat me! You'd be better off eating some chicken!

OKHLOBYSTIN: Wrong! Chicken is not better.

ZINA: You just think so.

OKHLOBYSTIN: What hands!

ZINA: (*Wipes her hands on a napkin*) What a maniac! Now what are you embracing me for?

OKHLOBYSTIN: No particular reason. For the beauty of the feeling.

5

ZINA: We don't need that kind of beauty.

OKHLOBYSTIN: You don't think so?

ZINA: Comrade Okhlobystin! I don't understand you.

OKHLOBYSTIN: Where do you live, Zina?

ZINA: Let's say – Lenin Street.

OKHLOBYSTIN: Maybe we could say something else?

ZINA: Maybe. Such as?

OKHLOBYSTIN: Let's say I'm going to kiss you.

ZINA: Let's say you won't get away with it.

OKHLOBYSTIN: Why should we say that?

ZINA: Because I'm not such an easy nut to crack.

OKHLOBYSTIN: Zina, Zina. I've had such a hard life. I've suffered so
   much, and now I've simply gotten old. But you …

ZINA: Everything will be all right.

OKHLOBYSTIN: May I kiss you?

ZINA: No. You aren't old at all. You're a wonderful person. You just
   drink too much.

OKHLOBYSTIN: May I kiss you, then?

ZINA: No. You have your whole life ahead of you. You will be happy.

OKHLOBYSTIN: Maybe you are my happiness?

ZINA: Don't make jokes like that.

OKHLOBYSTIN: I'm not joking. I'm going to kiss you.

ZINA: No.

OKHLOBYSTIN: Leave me some hope at least.

ZINA: Let's have a drink.

OKHLOBYSTIN: Let's drink to you.

ZINA: Everything is going to be okay.

They drink

OKHLOBYSTIN: You know what, Zina …

ZINA: What?

OKHLOBYSTIN: I'm still going to bite you.

ZINA: Comrade Okhlobystin!

AND THE GIRL LAUGHS, SHE LAUGHS LIKE A YOUNG GIRL
Ivanov looks at the Girl and smiles.

GIRL: Careful, I'll spill my wine.

IVANOV: Are you talking to me?

GIRL: Yes.

IVANOV: We are divided by an expanse of people and salads.

GIRL: Apples roll across the tablecloth as apples do!

INDEED, APPLES ROLL AS APPLES DO

IVANOV: Do you dance?
GIRL: Of course.
IVANOV: Do you smoke?
GIRL: I don't know.
IVANOV: Do you want an orange?
GIRL: Yes.
IVANOV: Do you want some candy?
GIRL: Yes.

ORANGES FALL FROM THE TABLE AS ORANGES WILL, AND ROLL ACROSS THE FLOOR

IVANOV: Take these apples, grapes, pears and ice cream and be happy
GIRL: Thank you
IVANOV: That's not the half of it
GIRL: How frightening
IVANOV: What's your name
GIRL: What's yours
IVANOV: Where have you
GIRL: What about you
IVANOV: That can't be
GIRL: That's funny

THE GIRL LAUGHS, EATS PEACHES AND THROWS THE PITS OUT AN OPEN WINDOW
THE BRANCHES OF BLOOMING PEACH TREES PEER IN THE WINDOWS THEY LAUGH AT
EVERYTHING

IVANOV: If today it wasn't
GIRL: Nobody would find out
IVANOV: Is that sad?
GIRL: It isn't if you don't know about it.
IVANOV: Color?
GIRL: Hazel. Sound?
IVANOV: Violin.
GIRL: Is that winter?
IVANOV: Fall. Is that laughter?
GIRL: Yes, and it's red, blue and very childlike
IVANOV: It's also what you know nothing about
GIRL: Or is it the wind, evening and rain?

OUTSIDE THE WINDOW THE RAIN POURS, THE RAIN POURS

IVANOV: Four-eight-nine-eight-three

NOTHING IS VISIBLE THE WIND HOWLS THE EVENING GOES DARK DARKNESS COVERS
EVERYTHING
SHADING EVERYTHING IN A DARK COLOR

GIRL: (*Laughs*) I don't know what I'm saying anymore

AND THE GIRL LAUGHS AND LAUGHS

and I don't know myself what's so funny what I found so funny I just
feel good and happy – the young girl laughs and laughs like young
girls laugh without stopping she can't stop at all this young girl is so
happy

ZINA: (*Loudly*) What a sad song. Do you hear that? What's it about?
OKHLOBYSTIN: All songs are about the same thing, Zina.
ZINA: What?
OKHLOBYSTIN: Once upon a time there lived two lonely people.
    A Man and a Woman.
ZINA. (*Hums*) "Two lonely souls happened to meet ... "
OKHLOBYSTIN: They met one day and each thought about the other.
    They spent a few days together ...
ZINA: Comrade Okhlobystin!
IVANOV: A few silent nights.
ZINA: Were they afraid of each other?
IVANOV: Each was afraid of losing.
OKHLOBYSTIN: They sat in the bathtub facing each other.
IVANOV: Gazing into each other's eyes.
GIRL: Thinking about each other.
IVANOV: Not about someone else?
GIRL: As friends will do?

They laugh.

OKHLOBYSTIN: And then they never met again.
IVANOV: They never even said anything.
GIRL: That wasn't that Man and Woman, was it?
IVANOV: She didn't come from my rib.
GIRL: It wasn't me?
ZINA: It wasn't me?

Okhlobystin invites the Girl to dance. Ivanov shouts after them.

IVANOV: I love Tanya! Tanya is beautiful! She sleeps on a velvet pillow,
    her skin is white, the velvet is black with night, a dark, cold night!
ZINA: (*Powders her face*) White skin.

IVANOV: Tanya is everywhere. Now and even when she is not here. Her eyes peer out from behind books in a room. Her eyes are beautiful, astonishing!

ZINA: (*Looking in the mirror*) Beautiful eyes.

IVANOV: She is in every aroma and she is in every one of my cells. Every centimeter of me has been kissed by Tanya, every centimeter has been kissed by Tanya.

ZINA: Every centimeter…

IVANOV: Tanya's warmth spans every distance. I sense it as a dog would a scent. Every step I take towards her breathes, every stride breaks into a run, my every breath hurries me on. I love Tanya!

ZINA: Every breath…

OKHLOBYSTIN: (*Shouts*) But she's so young!

IVANOV: (*Quietly*) There's something in this silliness, in this laughter of hers, in this nonsense.

ZINA: She's a serious girl. She talks about poetry.

IVANOV: She asks what I think about love. (*Laughs*)

ZINA: She asks something else, too.

IVANOV: I don't think so. But there's something in this, in her young body, in those slender arms. Maybe it's my happiness?

ZINA: Her name is Tanya, too.

IVANOV: What a coincidence.

ZINA: Give this girl some asters.

IVANOV: What if she doesn't like asters?

GIRL: What if I have some tea with him first? And then some cake, and then something to drink, maybe wine, and then, maybe, show a picture album, afterwards maybe?

IVANOV: Here are some asters.

GIRL: Thank you.

IVANOV: You like them?

GIRL: Yes. I love asters.

They are silent.

ZINA: I don't like them.

A VASE FALLS FROM THE TABLE AND BREAKS WITH AN EVENING-PEAL SADLY SQUEALING BEFORE FALLING FROM THE TABLE WITH A PEAL AND THE EVENING VASE – VIOLET AND PORCELAIN – BREAKS WITH A SAD PEAL

GIRL: How terrible

TVANOV: Tanya

GIRL: What

IVANOV: My wife is also Tanya
GIRL: I know
IVANOV: How
GIRL: I know everything about you, sir
IVANOV: Why so formal
GIRL: So there
IVANOV: Lock me away then
GIRL: What for
IVANOV: I'm a miscreant. I'll pervert you.

They are silent.

GIRL: Pervert me.

Zina and Okhlobystin collect the sad evening shards. Okhlobystin pinches Zina.

ZINA: (*Tempestuously*) Comrade Okhlobystin! I don't understand you!

Tanya

SCENE TWO

The Girl

Zina and Okhlobystin dance. Tanya and the Girl sit at the table. The Girl holds a bouquet of asters in her hand.

TANYA: It's so fun drinking champagne
        A third eye seems green
        A third hand seems useless
        When you remember you remember nothing
        And think you think nothing
        You walk down the street and shout. Happily. You're kissing someone.
OKHLOBYSTIN: Zina! I'll cover you with kisses!
ZINA: Comrade Okhlobystin!
GIRL: I was walking down the street eating an orange, throwing peels in all the puddles, littering up the town. Nobody saw me and I was not ashamed. I was happy. It tasted good and life was grand. I smiled and thought, "What a life!" Afterwards my hands smelled of oranges, and afterwards I had the feeling I needed nothing else ...
TANYA: A white road lies on the black earth and the house burns like a red sun. It's spring! Riding around Moscow in a black car and drinking champagne, now that's what I call fun!

OKHLOBYSTIN: In his time my best friend Guidon said to his future wife Klava, "Klava, you're an elephant. I love elephants. I always want to go up to them and crawl all over them."

ZINA: After that she married him?

OKHLOBYSTIN: Without batting an eyelash.

ZINA: Strange woman. He's no better.

OKHLOBYSTIN: What about me?

ZINA: You're a swine, Okhlobystin.

OKHLOBYSTIN: And you're an elephant, Zina. I love elephants. How can I not want to crawl all over you?!

ZINA: What a swine!

GIRL: (*Singing*) Sha-la-la-la.

TANYA: Dropping pebbles into a cup and playing happy tunes on a flute

GIRL: Look out the window at the trolley wires – the neighbors' windows say, "Look out the window"

TANYA: Who did you choose? Whose flirtatiousness? Whose eyes?

GIRL: You are very pretty.

TANYA: You are very pretty.

GIRL: I like you very much.

TANYA: I like you very much.

OKHLOBYSTIN: There was no prettier woman on earth than Klava until you appeared, Zina. I am at your feet!

ZINA: Oh, knock it off.

OKHLOBYSTIN: Klava's legs don't have a chance against yours.

ZINA: Legs like any other legs. Perfectly normal legs. What's got into you?

OKHLOBYSTIN: Believe me.

ZINA: (*Squealing*) Take your hands off me, Okhlobystin!

OKHLOBYSTIN: Zina.

ZINA: I'm warning you for the last time!

Zina leaves angrily, hiding her legs under the hoops of her skirt. Okhlobystin disappears after her.

GIRL: This morning I was riding the subway. He looked past me. He was taller and looked straight over my head. Squinting his eyes. He didn't notice me. I also looked off into the distance so that I wouldn't see he wasn't looking at me. I smiled a little and felt like an idiot. I felt so sad that he didn't care, that he didn't know anything, that in two seconds he'd be gone, that I'd get off the train before him, that basically – I didn't love him. I hated him.

TANYA: How did you meet?

GIRL: At somebody's house.
TANYA: Here?
GIRL: Yes. Just like you. He gazed into my eyes all evening long.
TANYA: What about you?
GIRL: Me? I smiled.
TANYA: All evening long?
GIRL: Yes.

They laugh.

    He's different with me. Not like he is with other women.
TANYA: Why's that?
GIRL: Because I'm special. I'm not like them.
TANYA: Do you love him?
GIRL: I can't live without him.
TANYA: Sometimes I think he's silly. He sits there in his chair, hunched over and muttering something. I look at him and think, that can't be him. That's not my man anymore. Or maybe its not any man at all. Your name is Tanya, too.
GIRL: Tanya.
TANYA: What a coincidence. I love my husband very much, too. We met on the beach. Great big dragonflies like that were flying all around.
GIRL: At the seashore?
TANYA: A bell rang but everybody was dancing and nobody heard it. I opened the door and he was standing there. We danced all night long.
GIRL: At somebody's house?
TANYA: He came running at me and nearly knocked me off my feet.
GIRL: Outdoors?
TANYA: He grabbed me, spun me around, set me down on the table and shouted, "Let's have a song for the most beautiful woman in the world!" The band played something very lively.
GIRL: A restaurant?
TANYA: I had to give him something in connection with my job, so I called him and we met by the movie theater. Then we went to see a movie.
GIRL: You mean it was at work, then.
TANYA: The subway. We saw each other and that's how we met.
GIRL: That's so cool!

They are silent.

    She poured tea (slowly) and spoke so gently
TANYA: Her blue eyes show the way (they are still trusting). I don't hear anything. I KNOW, THAT'S HOW HE LOOKS AT HER

GIRL: If only I could embrace her, tell her everything, be her smell, her color, her laughter
TANYA: I KNOW IT ONLY TOO WELL
GIRL: Erase all the years ahead so I could be her right now
TANYA: WHAT DO I DO NOW?
GIRL: The room smelled of her perfume
TANYA: Maybe I should poison her with something?
GIRL: Tanya
TANYA: Tanya
GIRL: You are very beautiful
TANYA: You are very beautiful
GIRL: I like you very much
TANYA: I like you very much

They take each other by the hand.

GIRL: My face
TANYA: my
GIRL: My hand
TANYA: my
GIRL: My body
TANYA: my
GIRL: How do you
TANYA: you
GIRL: How do I
TANYA: i

SCENE THREE

The Boy

Okhlobystin, Zina, the Girl, the Boy.

ZINA: I love you, Okhlobystin.
OKHLOBYSTIN: I'm not the one you need, Zina.
ZINA: I love you, Okhlobystin.
OKHLOBYSTIN: Zina, I'd be the end of you.
ZINA: No.
OKHLOBYSTIN: What do you need in a husband? You need a rich husband. I'm broke and empty-handed. And my name is Okhlobystin.
ZINA: It's a fine name for a kitten.
OKHLOBYSTIN: You've got such great legs you'd never be able to live with me. With legs like that, you should be walking on carpets of money.

ZINA: Have pity on me, Okhlobystin. I want to marry you.

OKHLOBYSTIN: It's not the time for it, Zina. I'm a destitute, impoverished man. Open your eyes, look a little closer.

ZINA: I always see everything even with my eyes closed.

OKHLOBYSTIN: Zina, Zina, Zina. I don't like talks like this.

ZINA: Sometimes they're necessary.

OKHLOBYSTIN: The kids are getting bored. Let's have a drink!

They drink, then are silent.

ZINA: Why don't people fly?

OKHLOBYSTIN: What are you going to ask next, Zina?

ZINA: If I were a bird, I would fly away from you.

BOY: You can't fly from love, you can't hide from it.

ZINA: Is that a song?

OKHLOBYSTIN: Zina, my sweet bird, you and I will sing yet. And we'll dance, too.

They turn on music and dance.

BOY: What do you see in the window?

GIRL: The window? Black smoke and a black smokestack. A single bright star burns in the black sky.

BOY: Like you?

GIRL: Like me?

BOY: Like the star?

AND THE GIRL LAUGHS, LAUGHS WITH RINGING LAUGHTER

ZINA: Why don't you have any money?

OKHLOBYSTIN: Money is like a bird.

ZINA: I would be happy as a bird.

OKHLOBYSTIN: Money disappears like a bird on the wing! It doesn't remember me, it sends no news.

ZINA: I would fly away somewhere.

OKHLOBYSTIN: And come back to me in spring.

ZINA: Do all women come back to Bibirevo in spring?

OKHLOBYSTIN: In spring all the birds return.

ZINA: I'm not your bird!

OKHLOBYSTIN: In spring even money turns up sometimes.

A TRAIN PASSING NEARBY DROWNS OUT THE VOICES OF THE SPEAKERS CARRYING THEM IN THE AIR AS IF THEY WERE A LIGHT RATTLING OF WINDOW PANES — SOMEWHERE FAR OFF WHEELS RATTLE BUT THE CURTAINS ONLY SASHAY A LITTLE

AND THE WIND BLOWS IN THE WINDOW CARRYING WITH IT THE VOICES OF THE SPEAKERS IN AN UNKNOWN DIRECTION

GIRL: Did you wave bye-bye to trains when you were a boy?
BOY: No. Never.
GIRL: Why not?
BOY: I threw rocks at them.
GIRL: How horrible.
BOY: I was a bad boy.
GIRL: I always waved bye-bye to them. And you know what? They would whistle back. Just for me.
BOY: That's nice. I'll bet you were a good girl. You want some more wine?
GIRL: Yes.
ZINA: Oh! Something just ran by there!
OKHLOBYSTIN: One of our little friends.
ZINA: Mice!
OKHLOBYSTIN: That's right, Zina. I have nothing against them. I feel sorry for them. They're so little.
ZINA: I'm afraid of them.
OKHLOBYSTIN: There's no need to be afraid with me.
ZINA: Oh, Vasya.

They embrace and leave.

BOY: Then they drank tea (she spilled her cup on the table and the tea spread out slow and hot, soaking into the newspapers, the matches and the books. We sat and didn't even lift our hands. We were silent.)
GIRL: The boy has a secret, the secret's in a box, the box is in a tree. Shoot it with an arrow and break it all to pieces. It's all so simple, no secret now.
BOY: She has blue eyes. Silent lips. I know how not to ask questions. That's the only thing she likes. She says, "It's nice that you're with me. It's nice that it's so simple."
GIRL: "Simple isn't good," he says.
BOY: I wipe the table with a towel. She peels an orange and holds it out to me. She says she cried yesterday – her tears were like these candies here. And then, she said, she thought, No.
GIRL: My tears were like these oranges.
BOY: Juice squirted in her eyes and her tears flowed.
GIRL: I said, Now they're just like these candies.
BOY: Now they're like huge oranges.
GIRL: Then it was morning. The room was dark, the way it is early. Yesterday's evening light crept down the wall. The Boy slept and dreamed – I caress his face and say, "I'm going. Sleep."

BOY: She caresses my face and says, "I'm going ... "

GIRL: I kiss him.

BOY: She runs her tongue down my body

GIRL: He scrunches up in his blanket

BOY: In the morning she smokes in the darkness (it's early morning, the windows are hung with curtains). I sleep, she kisses me and leaves.

GIRL: Then it's only him – he doesn't remember anything.

BOY: Then it's only her – she doesn't go anywhere.

GIRL: Then it's only us – we fall asleep together.

BOY: Only then, then, then.

The Boy and Girl run around the house, looking out all the windows, laughing and shouting.

Spring is insane! You are insane! Here – here are some flowers for you! There's no stopping me now! Keep your eyes peeled!

GIRL: Spring!

BOY: The sun today is already shining brighter than yesterday. The snow is melting. The wind blows warmer. Green leaves will soon appear on the trees. Birds will fly to our country. In the capital of our Motherland it will be Woman's Day, March 8. I will give you a tulip or a mimosa.

GIRL: Tulip

BOY: Or mimosa

GIRL: Tulip

BOY: Or mimosa

GIRL: Tulip

BOY: A bushy, yellow mimosa. It will stand forever somewhere on your dresser like a Christmas tree.

GIRL: What marvelous weather!

BOY: I'll give my sweetheart a Christmas tree!

GIRL: Spring!

BOY: I'll earn a ton of money! I'll go rake leaves!

GIRL: Leaves fall in autumn. Autumn is a long way off.

BOY: You'll dump me a hundred times by autumn.

GIRL: In the summer the poplars give off little fluff balls.

BOY: I'm a gardener. I won't let you lift a finger.

GIRL: Tell me another tall tale!

BOY: I'll kiss you.

GIRL: You'll get up at five in the morning and sweep and sweep and sweep.

BOY: No, at five in the morning I'll kiss you and kiss you and kiss you.

GIRL: I want that now.

BOY: (*Laughs*) You see, it's love.
GIRL: It's spring again.

SCENE FOUR

Night. Okhlobystin's house. The Girl sits in the room on a chair. Ivanov sleeps.

GIRL: I was thinking about your words
IVANOV: I'm tired
GIRL: I was thinking about how you talked about tenderness
IVANOV: It was a crazy day
GIRL: I was thinking about my tenderness
IVANOV: A madhouse
GIRL: I agree that that's the main thing
IVANOV: Sleep
GIRL: I want you to answer
IVANOV: Come here
GIRL: I want you to answer me
IVANOV: What do you want me to answer
GIRL: I don't know anything about you
IVANOV: You don't know anything about me
GIRL: I don't need anything from you
IVANOV: You don't need anything from me
GIRL: I just want you to talk to me
IVANOV: I did
GIRL: I hurt
IVANOV: I'm tired
GIRL: I'm going to cry
IVANOV: Don't
GIRL: So you'll pity me
IVANOV: Lie down, you'll freeze
GIRL: I thought about tenderness all day long today
IVANOV: All day long today I ran around town
GIRL: I thought about you
IVANOV: Tenderly?
GIRL: I was happy all day long today
IVANOV: All day long today I ran around town
GIRL: Today is the most horrible night of my life
IVANOV: I've got to get up early tomorrow
GIRL: I want to die
IVANOV: This little boy shouted obscenities at me in the subway – I was
  amazed

GIRL: (*Dressing*) That's funny
IVANOV: Lie down and sleep
GIRL: I can't
IVANOV: Where are you going
GIRL: I'm going to die
IVANOV: Calm down
GIRL: I hurt

The Girl leaves. Ivanov dresses and leaves after her.

SCENE FIVE

Monday

Okhlobystin runs around the house setting the table. He stands in front of the mirror a long time. He changes his shirt. He pours himself a shot glass of vodka and prepares to drink it. Enter Tanya. Okhlobystin offers the glass to her.

OKHLOBYSTIN: I'm leaving for the North. We won't see each other for a long time. Maybe never. What are you laughing at? At me?
TANYA: Of course not.
OKHLOBYSTIN: It's true. I'm leaving. (*Laughs*)
TANYA: I just came by the café and I recognized him instantly – he was sitting with the Girl, Tanya, there on the street at a white little summer table. It was cold, the wind was blowing and he took off his coat and threw it around her shoulders.
OKHLOBYSTIN: Sit here in this easy chair – that comfortable?
TANYA: He was in just his blue jersey with the 62 on it – that silly one.
OKHLOBYSTIN: Want some wine?
TANYA: With that stupid knit cap with the fuzz ball on top. I can't understand why he wears that thing.
OKHLOBYSTIN: It's very good wine.
TANYA: I sat down at the next table and they didn't notice me. They didn't even look in my direction, didn't see a thing. He
pulled his headphones
out from under his hat
and leans one ear up to hers
they laugh
he kisses her cheek
they smoke
he runs and buys her ice-cream
they listen to music

they laugh
he kisses her
they smoke
they talk
he buys her another ice-cream and then brings her some hot tea
they sit and warm their hands
they kiss
they laugh
and laugh
and laugh

OKHLOBYSTIN: Are you talking about the Boy?

TANYA: Yes. And she's very pretty, isn't she? She has beautiful eyes.

OKHLOBYSTIN: And he's a very nice Boy.

TANYA: White number 62 – on the front and the back...

OKHLOBYSTIN: Such kids.

TANYA: Both of them. So when are you leaving?

OKHLOBYSTIN: I wanted to today, but I'll probably go tomorrow. I'm going by plane.

TANYA: The cold wind twirls stray white papers around them, blowing them off the table. And they just sit there, with no reason to hurry anywhere...

They are silent.

It used to be I didn't pay any attention to young people. And now I go along the street and I see they're so young. They walk holding hands. My youth slipped away somewhere. In the subway I look at old ladies and fear I'll see their wrinkles on me. Old age is creeping up on me...

OKHLOBYSTIN: Tanya. I want to say one thing. Only don't laugh.

TANYA: Okay.

OKHLOBYSTIN: You're not going to laugh?

TANYA: (*Smiles*) No.

OKHLOBYSTIN: I love you. Is that so funny?

TANYA: No. (*Laughs*)

OKHLOBYSTIN: You happy now?

TANYA: Turn on some music. You've always got music on here. Today it's so quiet.

OKHLOBYSTIN: Have something to eat. Go on.

TANYA: Did you fix that yourself?

OKHLOBYSTIN: Yes.

TANYA: We can't eat all that, just the two of us.

OKHLOBYSTIN: We'll have to invite somebody over. Is that okay for music?

TANYA: Yes. You've got a nice place, here. So you're leaving tomorrow?
OKHLOBYSTIN: Looks like it.
TANYA: Would you rent me a room? If Zina wouldn't mind. I'd like to live here awhile.
OKHLOBYSTIN: Take any room you want.
TANYA: Thanks.

They are silent. Tanya looks out the window.

   Is today Monday?
OKHLOBYSTIN: Today is Monday. Wine. Headache. Tanya is sitting in my room and I still can't believe she came to see me.

They are silent.

TANYA: I've known it all for a long time. About you and about Ivanov.

SCENE SIX

Ivanov runs down the street towards Bibirevo. The Girl runs after him.

IVANOV: This is where I got in an accident
GIRL: How?
IVANOV: I only saw her eyes
GIRL: Whose?
IVANOV: We were dancing in the middle of the road
GIRL: (*Laughs*) You? Dancing?!
IVANOV: We were drinking champagne and dancing
GIRL: Who?
IVANOV: I love to dance
GIRL: I don't understand
IVANOV: We were looking at the stars. It was a warm night and we were dancing. Indescribably beautiful.
GIRL: Who?
IVANOV: The night. Tanya. And then all I heard was her cry
GIRL: Whose?
IVANOV: SHE LEFT ME
GIRL: Who?
IVANOV: Tanya
GIRL: What?

They come to Okhlobystin's house.

   I don't get it.

IVANOV: You will now. (*Picks up a big rock and heaves it at the window*)

Zina runs out of the house.

ZINA: Oh, my God!
IVANOV: Where is Okhlobystin – I'll kill him.
ZINA: Somebody broke our window!

Ivanov throws another rock at another window.

Comrade Ivanov, is that you breaking our windows? Are you crazy?
IVANOV: Where is Okhlobystin?
ZINA: He left.
IVANOV: Whereto?
ZINA: The North.
IVANOV: Where's Tanya?
ZINA: Right here. What are you breaking our windows for?! I don't understand you!
GIRL: Hello, Tanya!
IVANOV: You know each other?
GIRL: Yes. That's Tanya.
IVANOV: I know.

Okhlobystin comes out of the house.

ZINA: Vasya! Comrade Ivanov has broken two of our windows! Careful you don't cut yourself. There are pieces of glass everywhere – what are you still doing here?
OKHLOBYSTIN: Inclement weather.
ZINA: We've got to call someone. To put in new panes…
OKHLOBYSTIN: You're probably right.
ZINA: Comrade Ivanov, you'll have to pay for this!
IVANOV: Naturally, Zina.
ZINA: (*Looking through a phone book*) Vasya, what's that worker's last name? You know, the one we call Uncle Vanya.
OKHLOBYSTIN: I don't know. Workers don't have last names.
ZINA: (*On the telephone*) Uncle Vanya? Hello, it's Zina. Yes. Ivanov here has broken out all our windows. A trouble-maker? No. A friend. Well, he's jealous! Passion! No, not me, another woman. Yes. Will you come? (*Hangs up the phone*) He'll be right here.
OKHLOBYSTIN: What are we standing outdoors for? Come on in the house.

They leave. The Boy appears from the garden, looks at the broken windows in amazement and goes into the house.

SCENE SEVEN

Evening.

TANYA: The sunset tonight bodes rain – red as blood.

IVANOV: Does that mean rain?

TANYA: Well, whatever. It's a red sunset tonight. Marvelous.

ZINA: Red means wind.

GIRL: The dog rose has bloomed.

BOY: That means the perch are biting.

ZINA: I was chopping onions – my hands smell of onion. All day long. I washed them with strawberry soap but they still smell of onion.

TANYA: The sky is so clear; not a cloud in the sky. It's so stuffy.

OKHLOBYSTIN: It's a hot summer.

ZINA: Smell that. Smells of onion. And I washed them with strawberry soap.

IVANOV: It would be good if it would rain.

ZINA: Really fine soap, quite aromatic. How do they do that?

OKHLOBYSTIN: Maybe you'd like some more wine?

TANYA: I like drinking wine.

ZINA: And now apples smell like apple soap, and strawberries smell like strawberry soap.

OKHLOBYSTIN: Have a drink, Zina.

GIRL: I like white wine.

BOY: How about if I put on a record?

ZINA: But my hands still smell like onion.

BOY: I bought a new record. Listen to this.

IVANOV: Music like that also bodes rain – it's stuffy.

BOY: You just don't understand anything.

GIRL: That's pretty music.

TANYA: You want me to cry, don't you? Don't you?

BOY: No, not at all.

TANYA: I don't want anything sad.

ZINA: I can't believe how they smell of onion. Can I try using your perfume?

OKHLOBYSTIN: It won't help, my sweet, sad-eyed girl …

ZINA: What nice perfume. Such a sweet, sweet smell. How charming! What bliss it would be if the air was like that!

GIRL: I like that too.

TANYA: Just look at that sunset. Why is it you never see anything?

IVANOV: It's a very pretty sunset.

OKHLOBYSTIN: A very red one.

IVANOV: There's a deep blue strip running along the horizon.

OKHLOBYSTIN: It's a clear sky; no clouds at all.

IVANOV: It's stuffy.

GIRL: The dog rose has bloomed.

BOY: That means the perch are biting.

GIRL: If sparrows are flying low to the ground, that definitely means there'll be rain tomorrow.

IVANOV: (*Looking out the window*) I can't see a thing.

ZINA: It's probably too late. The sparrows are all asleep.

IVANOV: Who wants wine?

ZINA: I do, I do.

OKHLOBYSTIN: Zina, Zina.

ZINA: Zina what?

OKHLOBYSTIN: It's an old Russian custom – you don't drink wine when the swallows are sleeping.

ZINA: I didn't know that.

OKHLOBYSTIN: But you're arguing with me.

BOY: Go ahead and drink, Zina. The swallows aren't sleeping

ZINA: Why not? It's late.

OKHLOBYSTIN: (*Goes out onto the balcony*) Well, look at that! Ha-ha! Go ahead and drink, Zina! There'll be rain tomorrow! (*Shouts*) My Lord – there are swallows, God fucking damn it!

PART TWO

A Nasty Deception
It Gets Light

SCENE ONE

TANYA: It's getting light.

IVANOV: Some bird has been singing all night long.

OKHLOBYSTIN: It's not a nightingale is it?

TANYA: No. It's too squeaky sounding.

OKHLOBYSTIN: Maybe it's a goatsucker?

ZINA: I hope it's not a goatsucker.

IVANOV: Is that a bad sign?

ZINA: It's just not good.

IVANOV: Why?

GIRL: Maybe it bodes rain?

ZINA: It bodes no good.

OKHLOBYSTIN: What's it going to do – quit singing now?

IVANOV: Would anyone like champagne?

TANYA: It's so fun drinking champagne!

GIRL: What beautiful music!

ZINA: Did you buy a new record?

IVANOV: Music like that definitely bodes no good – worse than a goat-sucker. Isn't it, Zina?

BOY: You just don't understand anything.

TANYA: You want me to cry don't you? Don't you?

BOY: No. Not at all.

TANYA: I don't want anything sad.

ZINA: Goatsuckers might even bode death, I think.

IVANOV: Let's settle for rain.

TANYA: What wonderful perfume you have, Zina. It smells so sweet. How charming.

GIRL: The dog rose has bloomed.

BOY: That means the perch are biting.

ZINA: What a sunset today! Do you see how beautiful that is? And the air – what bliss!

IVANOV: The fog is rolling in. It's going to be a hot day.

OKHLOBYSTIN: Now the goatsucker fell asleep.

ZINA: There it is – the morning of a new day.

IVANOV: Would anyone like more champagne?

ZINA: Let's dance! Come, let's dance!

Zina leads Ivanov out to dance with him; the Boy dances with the Girl.

TANYA: When are you leaving?

OKHLOBYSTIN: Never.

TANYA: Why?

OKHLOBYSTIN: I lied.

TANYA: How humorous. And I believed you.

OKHLOBYSTIN: That's what I was counting on.

They are silent.

Every day I think about the fact that you are still here.

TANYA: Every day I walk by his house so he will look at me in the window.

ZINA: Comrade Ivanov reminds me of someone.

TANYA: The radio is playing in his room and he's smoking. I hurry by on my way to work.

IVANOV: (*To Zina*) She boards the trolley and I see her reflection. A piece of her overcoat, her face, a hand – she sails away, sails away.

TANYA: The whole day seems senseless and empty.

IVANOV: The whole day seems senseless and empty.

ZINA: Comrade Ivanov, you remind me of someone. Your appearance does.

OKHLOBYSTIN: Zina! Some man was calling you all day long today.

TANYA: I walk by his house in the morning and hope he will look at me in the window.

IVANOV: She runs past in the morning and doesn't even lift her gaze.

ZINA: What man is that, Vasya? He really called so early?

OKHLOBYSTIN: Maybe it was yesterday. Who is it? Come on, out with it!

ZINA: Lord, what a jealous beast!

TANYA: When I run past store windows I look at myself and think about him.

GIRL: What beautiful music!

BOY: The air is ringing!

TANYA: And the tram goes, "ring, ring, ring!"

IVANOV: She doesn't want to see me.

TANYA: As if we were playing cards.

ZINA: Maybe it's that sailor?

OKHLOBYSTIN: Last time you said it was a doctor.

IVANOV: It's slippery – she's afraid of falling.

ZINA: Vasya, he's a doctor in the navy! Was he from the North Pole?

OKHLOBYSTIN: He didn't say who he was.

TANYA: I'm always the fool.

IVANOV: (*Shouts*) Zina, I'm unlucky in love!

ZINA: (*Laughs*) I know, Vasya, it's my father!

OKHLOBYSTIN: Tell me another one.

TANYA: Okhlobystin, I'm unlucky in love.

OKHLOBYSTIN: What can you do? Me too.

BOY: Not me!

THE GIRL'S LAUGHTER SAILS ABOUT BIBIREVO SO LOUDLY THAT THE BIRDS TURN TOWARDS OKHLOBYSTIN'S HOME IN AMAZEMENT

TANYA: We're not talking about you or me.

IVANOV: This is silly, we're talking nonsense.

TANYA: About how mandarine oranges grow on trees.

IVANOV: Big huge trees grow right there on the street with big huge mandarin oranges on them.

TANYA: You can just go up and pick them.

IVANOV: There's no electricity in the subway.

TANYA: They sell flowers in the dark.

IVANOV: You're always looking at your watch.

TANYA: Every day I think you …

IVANOV: You board the tram and leave …

TANYA: I'm going to take a different route.

IVANOV: You're always looking at your watch.

ZINA: Comrade Ivanov, you know you really remind me of someone.

IVANOV: Shall we go home?

TANYA: Now?

IVANOV: Yes.

TANYA: (*Laughs*) I don't want to.

IVANOV: What do you want?

TANYA: You to leave.

OKHLOBYSTIN: Anyone for wine?

IVANOV: No.

ZINA: Strange.

IVANOV: I don't want anything.

ZINA: Nothing, really?

IVANOV: I'm probably just old. (*Goes out onto the balcony*) Oh, the birds are singing – CAW, CAW … (*Shouts*) WELL, HELLO, MORNING!

ZINA: What air … What air! What air …

SCENE TWO

When it Grows Dark

The Boy and Girl.

BOY: When it grows dark, when the grass along the road turns to silver dust

GIRL: When only this house is distant, when only when

BOY: At home a window is open and music and conversations are heard

GIRL: When men tell funny stories and women laugh and laugh

BOY: And then they dance, and the sound of conversations with senseless words are so mysterious that you want to listen from beneath the windows and peek in from behind the curtains

GIRL: It's so fine – just like in the movies!

BOY: So fine!

GIRL: So simple!

Maybe someone's kissing
Maybe it seems they're doing something else
Maybe everything may be just the opposite maybe

Italian music pours out of open windows
Maybe they aren't even saying anything to each other

If we were in a movie, I would sneak up on you on tiptoes
BOY: Your dress would flash by like red silk
GIRL: I would whisper to you quietly – I would hide behind you with my nose buried in your hair
BOY: You would almost be like smoke – you would fly away like one of Chagall's women
GIRL: I would hold a rose to my breast – I would sing down to you from above like a flute
BOY: I would think about my madness
GIRL: Would look around
BOY: Amazed
GIRL: Turning your head

The sounds of music, noise, shouts and the crash of breaking dishes are heard from inside the house.

BOY: Just a second. (*Runs into the house*)
GIRL: In the movies I would love you ...
VOICE OF ZINA: Oh, careful, careful you don't break that vase
VOICE OF IVANOV: Okhlobystin, you knew all along. You knew.
VOICE OF ZINA: Comrade Ivanov!
VOICE OF TANYA: He's got nothing to do with it
VOICE OF ZINA: He didn't know a thing, don't mix Vasya up in this!
VOICE OF IVANOV: I'll kill him
VOICE OF ZINA: Comrade Ivanov!
VOICE OF TANYA: Knock it off, now, knock it off
VOICE OF OKHLOBYSTIN: No, let's get to the bottom of this
VOICE OF TANYA: Zina
VOICE OF IVANOV: Tell him, go on – go ahead and tell him
VOICE OF ZINA: You get out of here
VOICE OF IVANOV: Then her and then you
VOICE OF ZINA: Everything is smashed – Everything
VOICE OF OKHLOBYSTIN: Get out of here, Zina
VOICE OF IVANOV: And you too
VOICE OF TANYA: Knock it off
VOICE OF ZINA: Oh, oh! Comrade Ivanov – you're going to have to pay for everything again
VOICE OF IVANOV: Calm down, Zina
VOICE OF TANYA: Somebody get him out of here
VOICE OF ZINA: Oh, Vasya, the tablecloth – Vasya

VOICE OF TANYA: This is impossible
VOICE OF ZINA: That is a very expensive piece, comrade Ivanov!
VOICE OF OKHLOBYSTIN: Come on, man! Come on, come on, come on!
VOICE OF TANYA: That's not true
VOICE OF ZINA: Don't hurt him! Careful!

*ECHOING THE CRIES OF THOSE MOVING AROUND IN SPACE, MORE DISHES QUIETLY
SMASH AND A PASSING TRAIN DROWNS OUT THE VOICES OF THOSE SHOUTING AND
CARRIES THEM OFF IN THE DIRECTION OF SOME OTHER TOWN WHICH FOR NOW IS
STILL WASHED IN CALM*

Ivanov runs out of the house and runs into the Girl.

GIRL: What happened in there? I …
IVANOV: I'm bad.
GIRL: (*Laughs*) I know.
IVANOV: I'm very bad.
GIRL: Yes. But what happened?
IVANOV: I'm a big swine.
GIRL: Okay.
IVANOV: What's okay about it?

They are silent. Shouts are heard from the house. We hear the Boy's voice.

   I don't want anything.
GIRL: So what?
IVANOV: I don't even want you.
GIRL: (*Turns away*) I don't care.
IVANOV: (*Stands on his head and then falls in the grass*) See? I don't even
   want to stand on my head.
GIRL: I understand. I understand everything.
IVANOV: You don't understand anything!
GIRL: I love you.
IVANOV: (*Laughs*) Thank you.
GIRL: My momma says …
IVANOV: Who says? Your momma? (*Guffaws*)
GIRL: What's the matter?
IVANOV: Momma! Your son is splendidly ill! Momma! His heart is on
   fire! Tell my sisters Lyuda and Olga[1]
GIRL: Tell who?

---

[1] This and some of the following lines incorporate quotes from Vladimir Mayakovsky's
poems, "A Cloud in Trousers," "Verses On a Soviet Passport," "Anniversary" and "To the
Whole Book" (the verse introduction to the collection, *As Simple as Mooing*, 1916).

IVANOV: He has no place else to go.
GIRL: I don't get you.
IVANOV: My dear little girl, don't be offended. Go away, get lost somewhere. I don't want to see you anymore, I don't want to!
GIRL: You mean that?
IVANOV: Yes!

The Girl runs away. Ivanov laughs.

Give me any pretty young thing – I'll rape her and I won't bat an eyelash – may every piece of official paper burn in hell ... ha-ha ...

READ THIS AND WEEP: I AM A CITIZEN OF THE SOVIET UNION AND TANYA DOESN'T LOVE ME ANYMORE

Let it all burn in hell ...
Your son has a fire in his heart ...
Your son is congenitally thick-headed, dear momma
Your son hasn't understood what's important in life
The most important woman in the world doesn't love your son!
NO!

Bursts into the house. Zina squeals.

IT ISN'T TRUE!
NO!
WHAT ABOUT YOU? WHY, BABY, WHY?

ZINA: Comrade Ivanov!
IVANOV: It's true – I was out and around handing out bouquets. It's not like I was stealing silver spoons from your drawers!
ZINA: What silver spoons?
IVANOV: I didn't steal any silver forks, I didn't steal any silver cups, plates, pens, knives ... WHY, BABY, WHY?
TANYA: Knock it off.
ZINA: What forks? What are you talking about? Comrade Ivanov!
IVANOV: (*To Okhlobystin*) Alexander Sergeevich![2] Allow me to introduce myself: Mayakovsky.
ZINA: What Mayakovsky? What is wrong with him?
OKHLOBYSTIN: Thanks for the poetry.
IVANOV: I'll tell you a secret: She doesn't love me or you, anyway. Imagine that. It's one thing she doesn't love me – but she doesn't love you either.

---

[2] Pushkin. One could say "Mr. Pushkin" in performance.

TANYA: I love Pushkin.

IVANOV: Who is this woman?

ZINA: You have had too much to drink today, comrade Ivanov.

IVANOV: I know, Zina. Will you drink to me? What about you, Alexander Sergeevich? I mean, I love you ... (*Kisses Okhlobystin*) You and Tanya. Imagine that. And nobody else.

Enter the Girl.

TANYA: What about her?

They are silent.

ZINA: The sun has shone brightly all day long today.

OKHLOBYSTIN: It's a hot summer.

ZINA: There's a beautiful moon today.

OKHLOBYSTIN: A white moon. A black sky.

ZINA: Ooo, something just flashed up over the roofs. Did you see that? It just flashed and disappeared.

OKHLOBYSTIN: Maybe it was thunder somewhere far off.

ZINA: What if it was a UFO?

TANYA: We need some rain.

ZINA: You see that luminescence? It must be some sort of electrical discharges in the atmosphere.

TANYA: It's growing light.

OKHLOBYSTIN: Some bird has been singing all night. Is that a goatsucker, Zina?

ZINA: How would I know? It's some squeaky kind of bird.

IVANOV: Anyone for more wine?

ZINA: Oh! Did you see that? Did you see that?

OKHLOBYSTIN: It's a clear sky; no clouds at all.

ZINA: How beautiful! You know, I am so happy!

GIRL: The dog rose has bloomed.

TANYA: Where is the Boy?

ZINA: Are we going to dance today? Somebody put on a record!

GIRL: It smells terribly of onion in here ...

They put on a record. The Girl goes outside and cries. Drinks water out of a faucet.

So what if I get a bacterial infection and die – no – so what if I have to go to the hospital and then he has to pity me. Let him cry his eyes out

Okhlobystin comes out of the house.

You'll save me, won't you?

OKHLOBYSTIN. (*Embraces the Girl*) It's all right. It's all right.

GIRL: I love him.

OKHLOBYSTIN: Everything will be okay tomorrow. Tomorrow everything will be all right.

GIRL: What if it isn't?

OKHLOBYSTIN: If it isn't, at least it won't be as painful.

GIRL: Lord, make me not love him anymore!

OKHLOBYSTIN: There's no escaping him for you. You are so young… And Tanya is not for him. Now, now. Calm down. Don't cry. You know I love you, don't you?

Enter the Boy, laughing.

BOY: You too, huh?

Zina comes out of the house.

ZINA: What's going on here?

BOY: Nothing!

ZINA: What are you shouting about if nothing's going on? I don't understand you.

GIRL: You're so mean.

BOY: Yes, sweetheart! Mean!

GIRL: And stupid.

BOY: (*Leaves*) Yes, my love! And stupid!

The Girl runs out in the opposite direction.

ZINA: Everybody is shouting today. What is going on? What is there to shout about, Vasya? Would you explain it to me?

OKHLOBYSTIN: It's feelings. Passions.

ZINA: Oh, my Lord! Would you look at that rain cloud! We'd better put rubber plugs in all the electrical outlets.

OKHLOBYSTIN: If we've got to, then let's do it.

They leave.

SCENE THREE

The Boy Invites Zina to Dance

Tanya's room in Okhlobystin's home. Ivanov is silent. Tanya reads a newspaper.

TANYA: (*Laughs*) I will be visited by love in June.

A knock at the door.

IVANOV: It's her.
TANYA: It's Okhlobystin.
IVANOV: He's come for you.
TANYA: It's only May yet.
IVANOV: July has been dragging on for two months.
TANYA: I'm not opening.
IVANOV: You'll be sorry.
TANYA: None of your business.
IVANOV: I want you.
TANYA: You always do what you want.
IVANOV: Because I always want you.
TANYA: Real men in love always do whatever the woman wants.
IVANOV: For example, stand outside the door.
TANYA: Real men in love always stand on tiptoe just a little.
IVANOV: I don't look like a man in love?
TANYA: All the men who loved me stood on tiptoes.
IVANOV: That's why you love me, not them.
TANYA: No.
IVANOV: All the men in love with you will soon go out of their minds.
TANYA: If he's still standing outside the door – I… (*Goes to open the door*)
IVANOV: You what? Well, what? What?

Tanya opens the door. Okhlobystin stands there with a bouquet of flowers.

  Hello, Vasily!
OKHLOBYSTIN: Fancy meeting you here!
TANYA: What flowers!
IVANOV: What a love! (*Leaves*)
OKHLOBYSTIN: (*Sits in a chair and long remains silent*) It's quiet…

Tanya fusses with the flowers.

  It's as if I didn't come by at all, didn't see a thing – didn't hear anything or say anything. Just as if I just went on by
TANYA: And flashed in the window?
OKHLOBYSTIN: Without thinking about you for even a second (or even less?). Or maybe I came in – but it wasn't me?
TANYA: This morning I was walking along the street and I turned around and saw I was walking along the street. Then I looked around again and saw my own turned head looking back at someone.
OKHLOBYSTIN: It was just a dream.
TANYA: In my dream I was lying on the sand sunbathing. Then I came up to myself and began looking over my body which was lying on the

sand. I ran my finger along my leg and saw that I opened my eyes and thought, "Who am I, then?"

OKHLOBYSTIN: Your soul.

Tanya laughs.

I dreamed the smell of milk, warm milk as if it were a recollection of something long ago. I smiled in my sleep. Then I opened my eyes. There was a child standing at the edge of my bed looking at me and he smiled too. When I smiled at him, he ran away.

TANYA: That was probably me in childhood. Momma always said that I smelled like warm milk.

OKHLOBYSTIN: And now?

TANYA: Now?

OKHLOBYSTIN: Now ...

TANYA: Now

OKHLOBYSTIN: Now

FALLING FLOWERS ARE AMAZED AT THEIR OWN FALLING THE WAY FLOWERS ARE AMAZED WHEN THEY FALL ON THE FLOOR UNEXPECTEDLY AS IF FALLING FROM SOMEONE'S LIMP HAND WHO DIDN'T GET AS FAR AS PUTTING THE FLOWERS IN A VASE GLUED TOGETHER FROM BROKEN SHARDS – THEY ARE SO AMAZED AT THEIR OWN FALLING

What a life we could have together – I forbid myself to think about it. I get suffocated just thinking about how inexpressibly wonderful it would be. And I forbid you to look at me like that, and I forbid you not to be with me. If you want to, let's get out of here – right now. I mean, time is passing, it's evaporating, it's vanishing, while you sit there getting around to realizing that you belong to me alone.

TANYA: What about Zina?

OKHLOBYSTIN: You are the exception to everything. You are the exception to all loves. You are love. It's our destiny that just you and I – we are everything, EVERYTHING.

TANYA: I love Ivanov ...

OKHLOBYSTIN: (*Laughs*) That's an empty sound, a myth, dust, your illness, jealousy, delirium – You ought to be whipped across the cheeks so you would quit fearing to name words with words, would quit fearing to ask simple questions when you already know what the answer will be

TANYA: I love Ivanov.

OKHLOBYSTIN: That doesn't mean a thing – absolutely nothing!

TANYA: Did you bring her here on purpose? Did you introduce them on purpose?

OKHLOBYSTIN: So what if I did?

TANYA: If it wasn't for her, everything would be all right.

OKHLOBYSTIN: No

TANYA: Yes

OKHLOBYSTIN: No

TANYA: Yes

OKHLOBYSTIN: No

TANYA: Yes

OKHLOBYSTIN: Tanya, sweetheart. I love you. Only you. I'll never love anyone again in this world as I love you …

They are silent.

I was walking down the street. It was snowing. There you were.

TANYA: I was walking down the street. It was snowing as I walked.

OKHLOBYSTIN: You were covering your face with your hands.

TANYA: You shouted, "I love Moscow and this wet snow …"

OKHLOBYSTIN: I wanted to spend my whole life walking up and down Sretenka Street, so that my whole life would become one funny little Sretenka Street, so that it would be – LIKE IT WAS THEN – you, snow, cognac, movies, the bookstore, dark sidestreets

TANYA: You really think it can be like that again?

OKHLOBYSTIN: I'll shout it at the top of my lungs

TANYA: I'm going home.

OKHLOBYSTIN: No, no, no!

TANYA: I'm going.

OKHLOBYSTIN: I won't let you. I'll hide your things. I'm going to lock you in this room. I … – I won't let you go – never, never …

Tanya leaves.

Tanya – Tanya – Tanya

Zina sits by the window. She heard everything.

ZINA: Betrayal! (*Leaving, runs into the Boy*)

BOY: Zina! Marry me!

ZINA: You all of you are so mean … (*Cries*)

BOY: Are you crying?

ZINA: You shouldn't make jokes like that.

BOY: Zina, I didn't mean to. I meant it seriously … Did I offend you?

ZINA: No, no. Everything's all right.

BOY: I'm not joking. Want to go to a restaurant? I've got money. Come on, let's go.

ZINA: To a restaurant?

BOY: We can go dancing.

ZINA: It's been so long since anybody invited me to go anywhere…

They leave.

TANYA AND THE GIRL PACE THE GARDEN LIKE TWO LARGE BIRDS, THEIR SHADOWS NEVER MEETING AND WITHOUT SEEING ANYTHING THEY FLY OFF AWAY FROM BIBIREVO IN SEPARATE DIRECTIONS FLAPPING THEIR LONG SKIRTS AS IF THEY WERE WINGS – THE WIND CARRIES ONLY OKHLOBYSTIN'S PITIFUL HOWL ABOUT THE GARDEN

SCENE FOUR

Okhlobystin Matures

Morning. Okhlobystin is alone.

OKHLOBYSTIN: Women follow me, peering out from behind branches and blades of grass. They gallop like does, squinting with their brown eyes, and then there is only a rustling, a whistle. There's no one there, only (what?); only me, only their former glances and a violin string humming and humming in the air until I close my ears and shout something at them. Until I fall in the grass and weep from exhaustion and nerves. Until I am suffocated by that endless confusion of love and strangled by my feverish sensations.
LEAVE ME, LEAVE ME ALONE YOU INTRACTABLE BEAUTIES, YOU NEFARIOUS WITCHES – MY LIFE HAS PASSED, MY YOUTH HAS ENDED, MY HEART HAS BEEN TORN IN PIECES BY LOVE FOR YOU, IT HAS FALLEN FROM MY CHEST AND GROWN UP AS A FLOWER. Now I will live quietly, diapering children, going for walks in the park, slowly smoking my pipe. FROM NOW ON ALL WOMEN PASSING BY WILL ONLY BE GETTING YOUNGER AND YOUNGER WITH EVERY YEAR THAT PASSES ME BY.
(*Shouts*) Zina! Zina! Zina! God damn it – where are you, bitter pill of my life? Zina! I have matured morally!

ZINA: (*Appearing*) What are you shouting about?

OKHLOBYSTIN: Zina, sweetheart…

ZINA: Lord, what happened?

OKHLOBYSTIN: Will you still be my wife, Zina?

ZINA: Vasya, what happened? Tell me right now.

OKHLOBYSTIN: Don't try wriggling out of it, you fool. I've just proposed to you.

ZINA: It's all so sudden, Vasya.

OKHLOBYSTIN: Zina, I'll quit drinking and everything else.

ZINA: Vasya, how can I put it…

OKHLOBYSTIN: I think everything will work out great for us.

ZINA: (*Wiping a tear*) Vasya, I…

OKHLOBYSTIN: You'll give me a little daughter. I really want a daughter.

ZINA: The fact is, we uh…I…

OKHLOBYSTIN: Don't cry, monkey.

ZINA: Vasya, I can't.

OKHLOBYSTIN: You can't what, you silly fool? Don't be afraid, I'm not lying. My mind is made up. I've been thinking about us all the time. About you and me. God's truth.

ZINA: The Boy and I…

OKHLOBYSTIN: What.

ZINA: The Boy and I just now, I didn't tell you…

OKHLOBYSTIN: What did the Boy and you just now?

ZINA: We just got married.

OKHLOBYSTIN: Oh, what an idiot… Oh, what an idiot I am…

ZINA: Vasya, are you crying or laughing? He really needed it badly – you know, to show everybody, to show them all. It was no big deal for me. He just needed a piece of paper, a document, some proof. I mean, you didn't want to.

OKHLOBYSTIN: I'll kill him.

ZINA: Vasya!

OKHLOBYSTIN: Don't touch me. (*Leaves*)

ZINA: (*Sits in a chair. Folds her hands on her knees*) Today I dreamed I took him by the hand. My feet rose up off of the floor. The light air carried us up to the ceiling as if we were helium balloons. He looked at me in amazement. I do love to amaze him. I said, "I have this power," but he still doesn't believe me. He doesn't believe me, doesn't believe me at all. Like a clown, like a young smart-aleck, he's satisfied with himself as he jokes… He holds me gaily by the hand and spins in circles all night long to his smart-aleck music which never existed before he did. He laughs. He makes me clumsy and he smiles just like a little boy! His gaze tells me, "Do you realize how sneaky I am?"

  I AM INSANELY SNEAKY

  I AM TERRIBLY SNEAKY

  I AM THE SNEAKIEST OF THEM ALL

(*She is silent*) That's all there is to it. It all happened pretty sadly.

(*Gathers her things and puts on her raincoat. Pulls a photograph of Okhlobystin out from behind the mirror, puts it in her pocket. Leaves without looking back.*)

The Boy races through the rooms, crying out in a long, drawn-out voice, "Zina, Zina, Zina." Then Okhlobystin comes in. He is sad and distressed and walks aimlessly about the house.

OKHLOBYSTIN: MY LIFE HAS ENDED – I'VE LOST MY SILLY, SILLY ZINA – SHE DANCES UNTIL SHE DROPS, NOTHING ELSE INTERESTS HER – SHE'S GONE GONE (*Sees the Boy. Stares at him a long time*)

BOY: (*Shrugs his shoulders*) That's right. Drunk.

OKHLOBYSTIN: So?

BOY: I'd even have to say, very drunk.

OKHLOBYSTIN: All right, Boy. Let's see your i.d. We're going to get to the bottom of this.

BOY: Why do you want to do that, comrade Okhlobystin?

OKHLOBYSTIN: Show me your i.d. It's for your own good.

BOY: I don't have an i.d. Yet.

OKHLOBYSTIN: What do you mean, yet?

BOY: On account of my youthful age, comrade Okhlobystin.

OKHLOBYSTIN: Are you kidding?

BOY: No sir. How come?

OKHLOBYSTIN: You little pipsqueak, what are you so drunk about?

BOY: I'm drowning my sorrows.

Okhlobystin laughs.

OKHLOBYSTIN: SHE DECEIVED ME! SHE DECEIVED ME!

Cranks the music way up loud. Shouts.

Dance until you drop! Everybody dance!

BOY: (*Dancing with Okhlobystin*) COMRADE OKHLOBYSTIN, I DON'T UNDERSTAND YOU!

OKHLOBYSTIN: NOTHING ELSE INTERESTS ME!

The Boy and Okhlobystin dance, punching each other, laughing and running about the room. The Worker walks about the house replacing the windows. He walks into the room and looks at the Boy and Okhlobystin with suspicion.

WORKER: One woman went out to empty the trash. Sees some guy on the trash heap looking for something. One thing leads to another and they start talking. He says, "I just got out of the slammer. Did my time, see, and now I can't find any work, any place to eat or anything to eat." So he's picking up old bottles and turning them in for the coin – at least it's something. She took a liking to him right from the start and he liked her, too. She was all alone just like him. And now they're together – does your heart good to see 'em. Ain't that a story?

OKHLOBYSTIN: Now there's feelings for you! That's real love! Everybody dance!

BOY: Uncle Vanya, have you been fishing for perch? Huh? Have you been fishing for perch?

OKHLOBYSTIN: They're really biting now! And she says, "He needed a piece of paper, a document, to show 'em all …"

They laugh.

WORKER: This woman was going home from a party. Everybody'd been drinking, naturally, and she was in a real good mood. She was walking along and she sees this young man lying in a puddle. Totally gassed. And it's really late already, and dark. But that didn't scare her and she took pity on the guy, helped him up and took him home. Next morning she finds out he's a really nice, shy kid! It was like, the first time he ever got drunk and he just fell there. You know, it could happen to anybody. And now they're together – does your heart good to see 'em. Like two peas in a pod. Amazing, ain't it?

OKHLOBYSTIN: You been fishing for perch yet, Uncle Vanya? Done any perch fishing yet?

BOY: Hey! Comrade Ivanov!

Ivanov stands in the doorway. He's holding a loaf of bread and a bottle of vodka.

OKHLOBYSTIN: What are you looking at? What are you looking at me like that for? What do you gotta loaf of bread, man? Put that bread down. Going around walking around with a loaf of bread. Where'd you get that thing? You need bread, huh? You need bread?

The Boy seats Okhlobystin on a chair.

IVANOV: I am so tired.

OKHLOBYSTIN: (*Sighs*) Well, pour me some, number sixty-two!

They drink.

IVANOV: I saw a lot of mice today.

BOY: You never saw any before?

IVANOV: There was a lot of 'em.

BOY: What about 'em?

IVANOV: They weren't real mice.

OKHLOBYSTIN: What are you looking at? What are you looking at me like that for? What are you always squeezing that loaf of bread for? You wanna eat? Then eat, man. And quit pawing that whole loaf of bread!

The Boy seats Okhlobystin on a chair.

(*Sighs*) Have some mushrooms. Zina pickled 'em. They're probably salad mushrooms. Have some.

IVANOV: There was just too many of them things. Too many.

BOY: Dreams are a bunch of nonsense – like the one where I buy a cat.
She walks down the street and turns around.
And I walk down the street and turn around
And the Girl turns and laughs
The cat laughs and leaves
She leaves and never comes back
She never comes back and everyone forgets her
Everybody forgets her and they start talking about
something new

OKHLOBYSTIN: What about mushrooming, Uncle Vanya? You been mushrooming in the woods?

BOY: (*Grabs the Worker by the lapels of his coat*) WHAT HAVE YOU DONE TO ALL OF US?! WHY DID YOU POISON THE MILK?!

OKHLOBYSTIN: So what about mushrooming, Uncle Vanya? Have you been mushrooming in the woods? Huh? I SAY, HAVE YOU BEEN MUSH-ROOM HUNTING? YOU BEEN MUSHROOM HUNTING IN THE WOODS?

IVANOV: So how come he poisoned the milk?

OKHLOBYSTIN: Who?

IVANOV: Uncle Vanya.

OKHLOBYSTIN: Yeah. That's Uncle Vanya. I know him real good.

BOY: INSANE VIOLINS FALL DOWN ON ME FROM THE HEIGHT OF THE FIR TREES IN THE PARK

OKHLOBYSTIN: Uncle Vanya, how come you put poison in our milk?

WORKER: I didn't put anything in your milk.

IVANOV: So then how do you know there's poison in the milk? Who told you?

OKHLOBYSTIN: She says – the Boy and I just got married ... (*Laughs*)

IVANOV: You're the one that did it, man! Snuck in the house like a mouse and poisoned the milk!

OKHLOBYSTIN: Man, how she cried ...

IVANOV: What you do it for, man?!

BOY: The water's boiling in the kitchen.

IVANOV: And you weren't the only one here, man. I saw you all! There was a lot of you guys here!

WORKER: I didn't put anything in your milk.

BOY: Hey guys, I feel pretty lousy ...

IVANOV: I thought you were mice! And it turns out, he's some Uncle Vanya!

BOY: (*Grabs the Worker*) WHAT DID YOU DO TO US?!

OKHLOBYSTIN: Come on, this is Uncle Vanya, guys. I know him. Hey, Uncle Vanya, you been out looking for mushrooms with the wife? Salad mushrooms, huh? I'm asking you – have you been mushroom hunting in the woods? Did ya get a good crop?

IVANOV: Oh, Uncle Vanya – and there I thought at first, I thought it's mice – that's what I thought…

OKHLOBYSTIN: What do you keep pawing that loaf of bread for?

IVANOV: Come on, admit it. Admit the whole thing.

WORKER: I did not put any poison in your milk.

IVANOV: Okay. So you didn't poison the milk. Right? What did you poison?

OKHLOBYSTIN: We ought to tie him up.

They tie up the Worker.

IVANOV: What did you poison?

OKHLOBYSTIN: So you don't go waving your arms.

IVANOV: What did you poison?

OKHLOBYSTIN: Ai, yai, yai… Walks by here every day grinning and then he goes and poisons us…

IVANOV: Let's at least make him tell us what he did it for.

OKHLOBYSTIN: And I even liked you, man.

IVANOV: What a scum.

BOY: Vasily, how is it that forty-year-old women got into our house?

IVANOV: You figure that? Guy sneaks in here like a little mouse.

OKHLOBYSTIN: Down with all women!

BOY: They're ducking in and out from behind the plates on the table.

IVANOV: I'll put him in the other room.

OKHLOBYSTIN: So you don't go waving your arms.

WORKER: I didn't go poisonin' nothin'.

OKHLOBYSTIN: What made you put it in the milk? How come not someplace else?

Ivanov carries the Worker into the next room. The Boy shakes the women from the table.

(*Laughs*) When's this all going to end? Do I want it to end? And what am I going to do when it all ends?
WILL I FEEL ANY BETTER FOR THAT?

BOY: (*Sits on the floor*) Daddy… Daddy… I feel really sick… (*Cries*)

IVANOV: (*To Okhlobystin*) I love Tanya.

BOY: i love Tanya

OKHLOBYSTIN: TANYA IS BEAUTIFUL

BOY: Tanya is beautiful
IVANOV: I want you to know that.
OKHLOBYSTIN: I KNOW THAT.
BOY: i know absolutely everything
IVANOV: And so that's the end of that.
BOY: and so – that's the end of that
OKHLOBYSTIN: THE END (*Raises his hands*)
IVANOV: I don't want to hear anything more. You got that? You got that?
BOY: i don't want nothing no more, nothing

Ivanov lifts the Boy off the floor.

    I imagined her voice ... – you don't believe me?
    in the nighttime sounds, hums and squeaks
    i rode it like a wave
    i sailed and listened to her laughter
    it fell and rolled down away from me, ran away and hid behind
    the door
    i missed catching it by only a second
    i arrived just a second too late
    i kept coming up late and i heard only her shadow
OKHLOBYSTIN: To your health!
BOY: Only her laughter – IT LAUGHED AT ME
IVANOV: Right now we are going to go to her and she will forgive us ...
    She will see us and forgive us ... She will forgive me – it's not your
    fault ... We're going to go to her right now.
BOY: I imagined her voice
IVANOV: We're going to go to her right now.

They leave.

OKHLOBYSTIN: (*Shouts after them*) SHE LEFT AND SHE'LL NEVER COME
    BACK!
IVANOV: (*Turning around*) Who?
BOY: Who?

They are silent.

OKHLOBYSTIN: Zina.

The Boy and Ivanov leave.

    My head is full of nonsense.
    Sometimes nonsense seems real wise.
    Oh well. I know how to wait.
    And there's time enough ahead to go nuts forty times over ...

(*Walks from room to room, gathering his things into a suitcase. Gets dressed and goes out. Locks the house*)
Well, time? Forward!

SCENE FIVE

Morning.
The Worker wanders throughout the house sadly looking out all the windows. But everything is closed. Everything is locked. A chewed-up rope hangs from the Worker's hands. The Worker breaks out a window, curses, climbs out and leaves.

WORKER: (*Stops and howls*) I'll poison every one of the sons of bitches!

SCENE SIX

People Love Having Fun On The Chermyanka River

Okhlobystin's house. Gay music is heard. Today might be a holiday. Zina flashes by, busy with something and humming. Okhlobystin sits in an easy chair reading a newspaper and smoking. The Boy prances from room to room, whistling. Everything is white and sunny – Zina's dress, the Boy's suit. The table in the large room is covered with a snow-white tablecloth and there are flowers all around. Tanya and Ivanov appear from the garden. Everyone smiles at each other and laughs.

TANYA: How nice it is here! So nice!
OKHLOBYSTIN: I have waited my whole life for some physicist to discover interim bosons – and now look at this, someone has!
ZINA: Is that in the paper?
OKHLOBYSTIN: Want some champagne?
TANYA: Hurray! I love drinking champagne!
ZINA: Everything's ready!

All sit at the table.

I had a terrible dream last night. It was like I was at some reception. I'm standing next to the table and I'm holding a big purse. Everyone is dancing and I'm shoveling food into the purse.
Then somebody says, "Check out what she's got in her purse!" And everybody looks at me. It was terrible. That's when I see the actor

Georgy Zhzhyonov standing there.[3] I say, "Comrade Zhzhyonov, tell them there's nothing in the purse!"

And Zhzhyonov takes me by the hand and gives me a ride home in his car.

I say to him, "Thank you so much, comrade Zhzhyonov – You saved my life!"

BOY: What did he say?

ZINA: Well, that part's not important, but can you imagine such a nightmare? You think it means anything?

IVANOV: I haven't dreamed anything for ages. I just drop off instantly into some black darkness – and that's the last I know of it.

BOY: Has anyone been perch fishing this year?

ZINA: Is perch the one with the red fins?

OKHLOBYSTIN: They're really biting right now.

ZINA: Vasily and I are going to the Crimea in August. He's going to write a scholarly report there.

TANYA: It's all so interesting!

ZINA: Yes. The correlating dependence of the form and structure of the ambulacral fields of walruses upon their lifestyle.

TANYA: I've never seen a walrus!

ZINA: I've never been to the sea.

BOY: Me either.

ZINA: Poor Boy…

BOY: (*Whispers*) Zina, you've got great legs!

ZINA: At your age the only thing that interested me was physics and geometry.

However, on the other hand, look how much time I wasted. I gave my whole youth to geometry.

And what for?

I love putting on a record, listening to music and dancing. The most important thing is to have a record and a record player.

That's all I need. We are going to dance today, aren't we?

The Boy and Zina dance.

BOY: Zina, there aren't any walruses in the Black Sea.

ZINA: Yes there are.

BOY: No there aren't.

ZINA: Yes there are.

---

[3] Georgy Zhzhyonov is a beloved Russian actor, suave, handsome, dignified and more than a little mysterious.

BOY: No there aren't.

ZINA: My Boy, that's just your jealousy speaking!

BOY: Ha-ha!

TANYA: Your perfume is delightful, Zina.

ZINA: Isn't it? It's like flowers.

OKHLOBYSTIN: Anyone for wine? Champagne?

ZINA: How I do love champagne! How I do love dancing! And how I do love music!

BOY: Anything else?

ZINA: I like everyone to be happy, to live in peace, and for no one to argue.

BOY: It doesn't happen like that.

ZINA: Basically, I just love people. And I love animals.

TANYA: It's probably wonderful in the Crimea right now.

IVANOV: It's always wonderful in the Crimea.

ZINA: I just can't wait to go there... I can't even imagine what the sea must be like...

IVANOV: I'm leaving for America.

ZINA: Oh, my Lord! So far away?!

TANYA: How I do love summer. Summer is always so pleasant and warm. I don't like snow. Summer in Bibirevo is so nice!

BOY: It's always nice in Bibirevo.

ZINA: They say it's nice in the Crimea, too.

OKHLOBYSTIN: Life is grand!

IVANOV: Yes, grand it is.

OKHLOBYSTIN: Aren't we getting on well?

IVANOV: Everything is just so fine.

OKHLOBYSTIN: We live well.

TANYA: I love it when all is well.

OKHLOBYSTIN: Oh, it's so good!

TANYA: It's nice drinking wine.

BOY: Yes, it is nice.

ZINA: But I hear things are bad in America.

OKHLOBYSTIN: Things are fine in America, too.

TANYA: How fine summer is in Bibirevo!

ZINA: They say things are nice in the Crimea...

Everyone looks off into the distance.

SCENE SEVEN

The Girl stands in the doorway.
Tanya turns around and spills wine on the Boy's suit.

BOY: Ahhh!
ZINA: Just like blood.

END OF PLAY

1 Ksenia Kutepova as Tanya in the Fomenko Studio's production of *Tanya-Tanya*, Moscow, 1996. Photo: Olga Chumachenko

2   Andrei Prikhodko as Okhlobystin in the Fomenko Studio's production of *Tanya-Tanya*, 1996. Photo: Olga Chumachenko

3 The Kutepova twins, Ksenia and Polina, as Tanya and the Girl in the Fomenko Studio's *Tanya-Tanya*. Photo: Olga Chumachenko

4 Polina Kutepova as the Girl in the Fomenko Studio's production of *Tanya-Tanya*, 1996. Photo: Olga Chumachenko

5 Andrei Prikhodko as Okhlobystin in the Fomenko Studio's *Tanya-Tanya*. Photo: Olga Chumachenko

6 Pyotr Fomenko and Ksenia Kutepova during rehearsals of *Tanya-Tanya*, 1996. Photo: Olga Chumachenko

7 Valery Kukhareshin as Okhlobystin. Vasilevsky Island Satire Theater, St. Petersburg. Photo: Olga Chumachenko

8 Valery Kukhareshin (Okhlobystin) and Darya Molkova (Zina) in *Tanya-Tanya* at the Vasilevsky Island Satire Theater. Photo: Olga Chumachenko

9 A scene from *Tanya-Tanya* at the Vasilevsky Island Satire Theater, 1996. Photo: Olga Chumachenko

10 Valery Dolinin (Ivanov) and Natalya Kutasova (Tanya) in the production of *Tanya-Tanya* by the Vasilevsky Island Satire Theater, St. Petersburg, 1996. Photo: Olga Chumachenko

11   A scene from *Tanya-Tanya* at the Vasilevsky Island Satire Theater, 1996. Photo: Olga Chumachenko

12   Viktor Shubin (the Worker) and Valery Kukhareshin (Okhlobystin) in *Tanya-Tanya* at the Vasilevsky Island Satire Theater. Photo: Olga Chumachenko

13 Students of the Fomenko Studio, under the direction of Yevgeny Kamenkovich, staged the first public reading of *YoU* at the Lyubimovka festival in June 1997. Photo: NG-Foto/Andrei Nikolsky

14 Polina Agureyeva as Pirogova in a student production of *YoU* at the Fomenko Studio, Moscow, 1997. Photo: Mikhail Guterman

15 Ilya Lyubimov (Seva), Natalya Blagikh (sister) and Andrei Shchennikov (Dmitry) in *YoU*. Photo: Mikhail Guterman

16 Ilya Lyubimov, as Seva, confronts Galina Kashkovskaya, as Yelizaveta Sergeyevna, Tomas Motskus (far right) as Stepan Ivanovich, and others in *YoU*. Fomenko Studio, 1997. Photo: Mikhail Guterman

17   Pavel Sborshchikov, center, as Barsukov in *YoU* at the Fomenko Studio, 1997. Photo: Mikhail Guterman

18   In Yevgeny Kamenkovich's production of *YoU* for the Fomenko Studio the entire cast shared the roles of the two old women. Photo: Mikhail Guterman

19 Olga Mukhina. Photo: Mikhail Metzel

Ю
(YoU)

CHARACTERS

STEPÁN IVÁNOVICH – *about 60 years old*
YELIZAVÉTA SERGÉYEVNA – *his wife*
ÁNYA – *20 years old, their daughter*
SISTER – *35 years old, their daughter*
SÉVA – *40 years old, Sister's husband*
ANDRÉI *(Andryúsha)* – *40 years old*
DMÍTRY – *20 years old*
PIROGÓVA *(Natásha)* – *20 years old*
BARSUKÓV – *50 years old*
NIKOLÁI *(Kólya)* – *20 years old, his son*
TWO OLD WOMEN

PART ONE

SCENE ONE

White Rolls-Royces, trolleys and flat-bed trucks race by Mayakovsky, Pushkin and Gogol. Morning airplanes fly above the ponds. Horses, bicyclists and pedestrians jostle with singing Mexicans. Lilacs bloom, it smells of rain, bread and salt. A huge sun shines over the entire city.
Seva and Andrei walk in the direction of the Kremlin.

ANDREI: I got two letters today. One from grandmother, the other from my sister. My grandmother's letter was incredibly tender.

SEVA: Careful there. Moscow does not believe in tears.

ANDREI: My whole life this city has observed me as coldly as a cold woman. A woman who laughs at me. Who never once offered me a hand, no matter how I whimpered or begged her to even just a little. I'm a stranger to her. I'm no one to her. She doesn't love me.

SEVA: All you have to do is throw money at her and she's yours all night long.

ANDREI: If only that were true.

SEVA: Your head spins, your ears ring, your feeble breast shakes with laughter. You bite your lips and swallow hard – and this town just begs for more!

ANDREI: I don't have any money.

SEVA: Moscow is not the world's bellybutton. Other countries have people in them, too, you know. You sound as little as Napoleon.

ANDREI: Every year it gets tougher and tougher. This town has stripped me bare. I hate it! (*Begins to cry*)

SEVA: Now, now.

ANDREI: I've got just one weary desire left in my head – to lie down here and die. To strip off these clothes, kick off my wet shoes, free myself of these rags and die naked – right here. Right here on this asphalt in the rain. I won't say a thing to her; I'll just think quietly to myself – HOW ABOUT THAT, SWEETHEART? I LOSE!

SEVA: Idiot.

ANDREI: I'm finished! Wasted!

Enter Pirogova. She runs and laughs and waves photographs in the air.

PIROGOVA: This is Vitya. He's a pilot. He took me for a ride in an airplane. Way up high! Way over Moscow! We even flew over your street.

SEVA: I thought I noticed something strange. It was like the weather went bad on just our street. But it was just Pirogova taking a plane ride!

PIROGOVA: We flew way up over the clouds!

ANDREI: What kind of plane does he have?

PIROGOVA: I don't know. I don't know anything about them.

SEVA: You going to marry him?

PIROGOVA: What's that got to do with it? He did propose, though.

SEVA: Accept. Go ahead.

ANDREI: I wanted to be a pilot when I was a kid.

PIROGOVA: When I was a kid I swam straight as an arrow.

SEVA: I drew swallows when I was a kid.

PIROGOVA: A swallow flew in my window once.

ANDREI: I don't like it when birds get inside.

SEVA: They say a nightingale flew into my room once.

ANDREI: So many birds flew into my room, I don't even know what they were.

PIROGOVA: Maybe it was a sparrow?

SEVA: Or something else, maybe.

ANDREI: What are you doing tonight, Natasha?

PIROGOVA: Where do you want to go?

SEVA: A greasy spoon.

Pirogova laughs and runs out on high heels.

ANDREI: What did you say that for?

SEVA: You never know what's going on in her heart.

They approach a small house and open the door. Inside music is playing. Anya, Yelizaveta Sergeyevna and Dmitry are sitting at a table and laughing.

DMITRY: I walk along the street and I can't do anything about it – I laugh! I love all those people who are walking past me, you know? It's like I physically love them! I want to kiss every one of them. I want to give them gifts, do something nice for them!

SEVA: Home at last.

YELIZAVETA SERGEYEVNA: Seva! Andryusha!

SEVA: Let's love each other physically!

YELIZAVETA SERGEYEVNA: Why so sad, Andryusha? You're probably hungry.

ANDREI: You think that's what I came here for?

YELIZAVETA SERGEYEVNA: Of course not. I just always want you to have a full stomach.

ANDREI: Thank you. I got two letters today. One from grandma and one from my sister. I decided to read grandma's first. I figured she'd be criticizing and ridiculing me. Then I'd read my sister's letter, to save the best for last. But grandma wrote me such a tender letter I even cried.

ANYA: I think it's horrible when a man cries.

ANDREI: Yeah. I was walking down the street thinking I'd die if I didn't have a drink.

YELIZAVETA SERGEYEVNA: Did you?

ANDREI: I had to. So I wouldn't die.

YELIZAVETA SERGEYEVNA: It's the other way around with me. I think if I die I'll never drink again. So I guess I'd better not die.

SEVA: That gives you some kind of goal in life anyway.

ANYA: I keep getting love letters from someone in violet ink.

SEVA: How romantic!

ANYA: Do you know anybody with handwriting as ugly as this?

ANDREI: No, I don't. What are you drinking? Wine?

ANYA: Yes. Dmitry's home.

SEVA: For long?

DMITRY: Yes, if there's no war.

YELIZAVETA SERGEYEVNA: Whenever I see those boys I feel so sorry for them. I want to do something for them. I want to help. I want to go up to them and say, "Everything is going to be all right."

ANYA: He's not one of them.

DMITRY: I'm happy.

ANYA: He smiles in the bus at grown-up women he doesn't know.

DMITRY: I like life. I think I can do anything I want.

ANDREI: He looks like a hero.

ANYA: That's what everybody says.

SEVA: Welcome home!

Everyone laughs and drinks.

DMITRY: Moscow has completely changed. I went into the post office and a pretty girl was eating grapes. She smiled at me, stamped my envelope and laughed. That didn't used to happen.

SEVA: Girls didn't used to smile at you?

DMITRY: No.

SEVA: (*Laughs*) There it is – the honest face of youth!

ANDREI: What else have you noticed in our city?

DMITRY: They are planting trees everywhere.

YELIZAVETA SERGEYEVNA: They'll plant trees and paint the buildings and fix the roads. Then it will be just like before the war.

ANYA: I hope it happens soon!

YELIZAVETA SERGEYEVNA: What a time that was! How we danced! I used to lose ten pounds after every dance! Ten, hell! Twenty!

ANDREI: What a nice past you had.

SEVA: Maybe we ought to dance?

YELIZAVETA SERGEYEVNA: I've probably forgotten how.

SEVA: I don't believe you! (*Grabs Yelizaveta Sergeyevna*)

ANYA: Careful, Seva! Careful!

ANDREI: Bravo!

Anya and Dmitry drink wine, dreamily looking out over Moscow, its lights, streets and cars. Andrei re-reads his letters.

DMITRY: Everything is so beautiful! You are beautiful. Moscow is beautiful.

ANYA: I'm dying to be so incredibly beautiful that everyone will lose their head!

DMITRY: In that case you are just as beautiful as Moscow.

ANYA: No! Moscow is old!

DMITRY: But you are incredibly beautiful.

Anya laughs.

How was it here without me?

ANYA: I've already forgotten how old you are.

DMITRY: I'm twenty. I'm already a full-grown young man.

ANYA: I'm twenty and I've never been to a foreign country.

DMITRY: There's no winter there.

ANYA: I don't like winter.

DMITRY: I didn't think of anything but you.

ANYA: When you left you looked like a plucked chicken.

DMITRY: What about now?

ANYA: Now, too.

DMITRY: Now I look like a hero. That's what everybody says.

Anya laughs.

I wandered up and down the boulevards during the night. It was dark and quiet and everybody on the benches was kissing – the air was swimming in love! In the daytime flowers are on sale everywhere.

ANYA: Didn't it used to be like that?

DMITRY: I always want to buy lots of bouquets and hand them out to all the girls.

SEVA: Pirogova says that's all men are good for.
DMITRY: I saw her yesterday.
YELIZAVETA SERGEYEVNA: Did you give her any flowers?
DMITRY: No. She disappeared too quick.
SEVA: Maybe she got scared.
DMITRY: Yeah. I shouted really loud and then gave her a big, long kiss.
ANYA: I bet she hadn't kissed anyone in a hundred years.
DMITRY: What about you?
ANYA: What about you?
DMITRY: You cried when I left.
ANYA: I always cry when someone leaves.
YELIZAVETA SERGEYEVNA: Let's have some tea or coffee!
SEVA: Tea or coffee?
ANDREI: Tea.
ANYA: Or coffee?

They laugh and shift around the cups.

DMITRY: I've been dreaming of this city for so long! Just to be able to stand somewhere and wait for a trolley – and nothing more. So my heart would feel joy and my soul would exult! To stand in a quiet snow or bask in a rosy sunset. To watch girls dancing and dogs running down the middle of the road. I really wish winter would come!
YELIZAVETA SERGEYEVNA: I don't want winter to come.
DMITRY: I really love this city.
ANDREI: I love this city too.
DMITRY: I love my country.
ANYA: I love it too. So what of it?
SEVA: That's good.
DMITRY: I was afraid maybe you'd quit loving it. You... You're just like... You're like you were before... You're just like then...
ANYA: No. I'm happy my childhood has passed.
YELIZAVETA SERGEYEVNA: I spent my whole childhood riding my bicycle in Petrovsky Park!
ANDREI: I had an orange cat when I was a kid.
ANYA: I had a pink cat.
DMITRY: When I was a kid I lost a game of ping-pong to my girlfriend.
SEVA: My girlfriend taught me to light matches.
DMITRY: Back there everybody was asking me, "Where are you going?"
SEVA: To Moscow.
YELIZAVETA SERGEYEVNA: And they said, "Oh..."

All laugh.

DMITRY: I'd say – MOSCOW ISN'T AS FAR AS YOU THINK YOU JUST HAVE TO WANT TO BE THERE.

ANDREI: But Moscow doesn't love everybody. It doesn't greet everybody with open arms. It doesn't forgive everybody.

DMITRY: It greeted me with open arms. And a big, happy smile.

ANDREI: You think so?

DMITRY: I know so. I can feel the sun shining up ahead.

SCENE TWO

Enter Sister.

SISTER: There's shooting in the street. You hear that?

SEVA: This is my wife.

DMITRY: Dmitry.

ANYA: Careful a breeze doesn't knock you over.

YELIZAVETA SERGEYEVNA: Is that the wind or is somebody knocking?

SEVA: I think someone's at the door.

Enter Pirogova.

PIROGOVA: No, that was just me catching my hand on a stray nail.

YELIZAVETA SERGEYEVNA: Oh, come in, Natasha.

SISTER: You hear that?

PIROGOVA: (*Gaily*) Shooting!

ANYA: It's right here.

PIROGOVA: It's Vitya. He's a pilot.

YELIZAVETA SERGEYEVNA: He's shooting out of an airplane?

PIROGOVA: He's firing his rifle out of jealousy. Only don't tell him I'm here.

ANYA: What a life! Young pilots shooting off their rifles in the streets, going out of their minds with jealousy!

Gunfire and shouts of "Natasha! Natasha!" are heard outside the window.

YELIZAVETA SERGEYEVNA: Pirogova, sweetheart, what did you do to him?

SEVA: Another good man goes down.

ANDREI: What kind of a rifle does he have?

PIROGOVA: I don't know. I don't know anything about them.

SISTER: Is this pilot good-looking?

PIROGOVA: Yes.

ANYA: He's a demon!

YELIZAVETA SERGEYEVNA: Now, Anya.

SISTER: I saw a falling star today. I made a wish.

SEVA: What did you wish?

SISTER: Don't ask.

ANDREI: You always look up at the sky with hope in summer.

YELIZAVETA SERGEYEVNA: The Big Dipper's over our street.

SISTER: It makes your head spin!

PIROGOVA: I killed a cockroach this morning and washed it down the drain.

ANYA: I'm in a silly mood today, too!

DMITRY: Moscow is completely different. I walked home on tiptoes through all the familiar streets of my hometown. I lay down on a bench on the boulevard, looked up at the sky and cried. Back there I didn't cry once. But here I burst into tears for everything put together, for everything.

SISTER: I don't ever cry.

All look at the sky. Dmitry and Sister look at each other.

It's like a dream. Just him and me.

DMITRY: It's just her and me by the blue window. She speaks words and the fog carries them away.

SISTER: The evening looks like your favorite color.

Barsukov appears in the doorway. He removes his hat and wipes tears from his face.

BARSUKOV: Is there…?

SEVA: No. We've only got wine, Barsukov. You don't drink that.

DMITRY: She heard the word "wine" and turned her head.

PIROGOVA: He's probably hungry.

BARSUKOV: Is there an adult in here?

DMITRY: Seva always forgot his lighted cigarettes and lit up new ones.

YELIZAVETA SERGEYEVNA: What's happened this time?

BARSUKOV: Kolya's been arrested.

YELIZAVETA SERGEYEVNA: What? What for?!

BARSUKOV: My poor boy…

Two old women peek out from behind his back.

FIRST OLD WOMAN: Look – there's Kolya.

SECOND OLD WOMAN: And there's Kolya.

FIRST: And here's Kolya.

SECOND: Here and here and here.

FIRST: Look at all of them.

SECOND: Ich nicht.
FIRST: There's more and more and more.
SECOND: Ach, mein Gott.
FIRST: Kolya, Kolya, Kolya.
SECOND: Don't call him. Don't call him. (*Disappears into the corridor*)
YELIZAVETA SERGEYEVNA: How did it happen?
BARSUKOV: I don't know.
SEVA: Let's go, Barsukov.
YELIZAVETA SERGEYEVNA: How unpleasant!
ANYA: Poor Kolya.
ANDREI: I'll go with you.
PIROGOVA: I've never been to the police.

All leave except for Dmitry and Sister who are alone.

DMITRY: It all happened very strangely. I simply touched her and she touched me.

SCENE THREE

Dancing Leads To No Good

Dmitry and Sister.

DMITRY: I remember you. We played cards when I was a kid.
SISTER: I remember you, too.
DMITRY: So many years gone by and you're still just as pretty. I thought you must already be so old.
SISTER: And I thought you were still a little pipsqueak.
DMITRY: I'm not a pipsqueak.
SISTER: I'm not old.
DMITRY: Will you dance with me?
SISTER: No.
DMITRY: Because I'm drunk, is that it? It's just a little. I don't ever overdo it.
SISTER: I don't care.
DMITRY: My whole life I've dreamed of growing up and dancing with Anya's Sister.
SISTER: No.
DMITRY: Why?
SISTER: Because you'll start chasing after me. I'll get tired of you and you'll go whimpering.
DMITRY: No I won't.

SISTER: Yes you will.

AND THEN THEY DANCED

DMITRY: Let's go for a walk! We can sit on a bench and hold hands!
SISTER: (*Laughs*) Only to keep from falling. This strange boulevard always makes me feel drunk!
DMITRY: Or we can go shrieking at the seagulls and throw handfuls of bread to them! Then I'll rip my heart out of my chest and drown it in the gray Moscow waters.
SISTER: You make me laugh!
DMITRY: I do?
SISTER: You do.
DMITRY: Why?
SISTER: You put a bull's-eye on your chest – right where your heart is!

They leave.

SCENE FOUR

Stepan Ivanovich walks about the room lost in thought. He listens to the radio and drinks. Enter a young man in a white suit.

NIKOLAI: Hello, Stepan Ivanovich. Am I intruding?
STEPAN IVANOVICH: Of course not. Come in, Kolya.
NIKOLAI: Can you give me a loan, Stepan Ivanovich?
STEPAN IVANOVICH: Wine? Women? Drugs?
NIKOLAI: Love.
STEPAN IVANOVICH: That one's sacred.
NIKOLAI: It's Anya. Whenever she swims the crawl or the breast-stroke her sun-tanned body sparkles like a golden fish. I've got love like love never happens! Endless! Magnificent!
STEPAN IVANOVICH: Hopeless. (*Gives Nikolai some money*)
NIKOLAI: Why?
STEPAN IVANOVICH: You're too late. She's already got a friend. He looks like a hero. That's what everybody says.
NIKOLAI: Bull. I'll have one of my friends kill him.
STEPAN IVANOVICH: You'll go to jail, Kolya.
NIKOLAI: He'll kill him, not me.
STEPAN IVANOVICH: Oh, Kolya, Kolya. (*Pours drinks for both and they drink*)
NIKOLAI: Thank you, Stepan Ivanovich! You're a kid's best friend! (*Leaves*)

STEPAN IVANOVICH: (*Thoughtfully*)
FUZZY WUZZY SAILED A BOAT
WRAPPED UP IN A SAILOR'S COAT
NOW THERE'S A REASON STRAIGHT AND TRUE
TO HAVE MYSELF A DRINK OR TWO.

Stepan pours a drink and downs it. In the corridor we hear the laughter of Yelizaveta Sergeyevna and the voice of Barsukov. Stepan Ivanovich hides his radio.

YELIZAVETA SERGEYEVNA: (*Enters, kisses Stepan Ivanovich*) We were out walking on the hillside and took a swim in the river!

BARSUKOV: The water in the river is warm and clean this year.

YELIZAVETA SERGEYEVNA: If you go out early in the morning and stand quietly by the bank you can see at least ten different kinds of river fish!

BARSUKOV: You can see the underwater plants and grasses very clearly, too.

YELIZAVETA SERGEYEVNA: If you stand there long enough and look very carefully you can even see little tiny animals.

BARSUKOV: Mythical little hunchback horses, tadpoles and other little maggots like that.[1]

STEPAN IVANOVICH: There used to be sprats flying around down there. They would hang in the air just above your head and you could catch them and eat them.

BARSUKOV: It was a good time.

STEPAN IVANOVICH: You're telling me.

BARSUKOV: Any news on the radio?

YELIZAVETA SERGEYEVNA: Oh! I don't want to hear about it! This summer we're living without calendars. We're going to focus ourselves on apples, cucumbers and blooming trees.

BARSUKOV: How's the harvest throughout the country this year?

STEPAN IVANOVICH: The harvest? What's there to harvest?

YELIZAVETA SERGEYEVNA: It's all lies!

STEPAN IVANOVICH: Where were you all night?

YELIZAVETA SERGEYEVNA: At the police station.

STEPAN IVANOVICH: Was that the best you could do?

BARSUKOV: Let me explain. My son was out walking his dog.

YELIZAVETA SERGEYEVNA: On Red Square!

BARSUKOV: Such a nice dog and so many problems!

---

[1] "The Little Hunchback Horse" is a classic folk tale.

YELIZAVETA SERGEYEVNA: It bit a policeman.
STEPAN IVANOVICH: Bad?
YELIZAVETA SERGEYEVNA: As bad as it could.

Enter Seva and Andrei.

SEVA: Is our dog-keeper here yet?
YELIZAVETA SERGEYEVNA: Seva, Andryusha. You look so sad again.
ANDREI: I can't help what my face looks like.
YELIZAVETA SERGEYEVNA: Have an apple.
SEVA: He already ate a peach.
BARSUKOV: You know what? I've noticed people in Moscow all chew
    with their front teeth.
STEPAN IVANOVICH: Anybody specific you have in mind?
BARSUKOV: You're just used to it and you don't notice it. But I'm
    telling you – everybody in Moscow chews with their front teeth!
    I noticed that a long time ago.
STEPAN IVANOVICH: What a bunch of nonsense!
YELIZAVETA SERGEYEVNA: Only let's don't start raising serious
    questions.
SEVA: Why not?
ANDREI: BECAUSE YOUR CONVERSATIONS UNFURL LIKE STREAMERS BEFORE MY
    EYES AND ALL YOUR MOSCOW IS NOTHING BUT A TERRIBLE DREAM – MEANWHILE
    MY OWN HEART HERE IS ROCKING ME TO AND FRO
YELIZAVETA SERGEYEVNA: Are you feeling all right?
ANDREI: Yes.
SEVA: He's dying here!
BARSUKOV: Dying?
YELIZAVETA SERGEYEVNA: Have a drink. (*Pours*)
BARSUKOV: That make it better?
STEPAN IVANOVICH: That always makes it better.
YELIZAVETA SERGEYEVNA: You probably don't eat much.
ANDREI: I can't get any air!
SEVA: What kind of air do you need?
ANDREI: There's no air! No air! No air! (*Runs out, knocking Anya over as
    she comes in the door*)
ANYA: What's he shouting about?
SEVA: He's got love on his mind.
YELIZAVETA SERGEYEVNA: I warned you!
ANYA: Love?
SEVA: About how deceitful it is.
YELIZAVETA SERGEYEVNA: Why don't we have some tea?

BARSUKOV: Many years ago I drank tea in a café. There was a girl there,very pretty. Every morning I drank tea there and talked with her about the weather. Then one day I went to another café and there she was sitting on some Chinaman's knee.

STEPAN IVANOVICH: So?

BARSUKOV: That's all I've got to say about love.

YELIZAVETA SERGEYEVNA: My heart even skipped a beat.

STEPAN IVANOVICH: So are you going to have some tea or are you going to leave?

BARSUKOV: Come to think of it – it's high time. (*Leaves*)

YELIZAVETA SERGEYEVNA: What happened to all our cups?

Enter Pirogova.

PIROGOVA: What are those old women doing out there sleeping in the corridor?

YELIZAVETA SERGEYEVNA: They'll go away soon.

SEVA: What are they always doing here?

STEPAN IVANOVICH: They've become part of the scenery.

YELIZAVETA SERGEYEVNA: You talk as if they bother somebody. They just sleep quietly in the corridor, that's all.

STEPAN IVANOVICH: And then things start disappearing.

PIROGOVA: What things?

YELIZAVETA SERGEYEVNA: Those little red cups.

ANYA: Which are orange.

PIROGOVA: Maybe they broke?

YELIZAVETA SERGEYEVNA: That would be the end of me. (*Goes to look for the cups; Stepan Ivanovich goes with her*)

ANYA: I think I'll drink some wine. (*Lights a cigarette*)

PIROGOVA: Smoking will make you grow a moustache.

ANYA: And wine makes you grow a beard?

PIROGOVA: It's how the female body works.

ANYA: (*Laughs*) I have this feeling I was drunk throughout my whole childhood!

SEVA: Great childhood.

ANYA: Mom would send me to the store for kerosene and say, "Now don't talk to strangers." Then some guy on a motorcycle would come up and offer me a ride. I'd get up there with him and I'd speed on after my kerosene staring into his black leather back. He'd say, "What's your name," and I'd lie. I'd tell him my name was Masha. Mom would ask, "How'd you get back so fast?" But my lips were sealed. I wouldn't say a thing about going to the movies with the guy on the motorcycle.

Otherwise she would have let me have it. That young motorcycle guy was so handsome!

PIROGOVA: What's the good of remembering him now?

ANYA: I LOVE YOUNG MEN I LOVE HANDSOME MEN I LOVE REAL MEN

PIROGOVA: The main thing is to love with your head, too. Not just with your heart.

SEVA: Right on, Pirogova!

ANYA: You don't understand anything, Pirogova!

PIROGOVA: Says who? I love horses, lakes, flowers and forests.

SEVA: What about that pilot?

PIROGOVA: What, may I ask, do you care for?

SEVA: Well...

PIROGOVA: What is that blooming under your window, a lime-tree? I wonder, what do lime-trees smell like when they bloom? Lilac, maybe? (*Opens the window*)

ANYA: All those people walking down the street and not a single familiar face. Strange, isn't it?

SEVA: I'm used to it.

PIROGOVA: Look! She was kissing his hands!

ANYA: Who?

SEVA: What nonsense.

Dmitry and Sister stand beneath the window.

SISTER: We went to the movies.

SEVA: I suspected you were capable of something like that.

SCENE FIVE

The Old Women dance around the room.

FIRST OLD WOMAN: We were out and around choosing flour

SECOND OLD WOMAN: Spitting on our fingers and rolling it into balls

FIRST: We tried it on the tip of our tongues

SECOND: We blew it off our palms

FIRST: White, white flour

PIROGOVA: JUST LIKE SNOW

SECOND: Good, good flour

FIRST: Yeast batter

SECOND: One to two or one to three if twice as much

FIRST: On the tip of a knife

SECOND: And half an eggshell of water
FIRST: Plus a little pinch
SECOND: Two parts to one
FIRST: A cup of milk
SECOND: We'll heat up the oven
FIRST: And make some meat pies
SECOND: We'll have a wedding
ANYA: ARE WE GOING TO DRINK WINE?
SISTER: ONLY A LITTLE
FIRST: Dance some dances
PIROGOVA: DANCES LEAD TO NO GOOD
FIRST: We'll make meat pies out of white flour
SECOND: And some whole wheat bread
DMITRY: THEN LET THEM RISE
SEVA: THEN LET THEM STAND
FIRST: Let 'em, let 'em, let 'em
SECOND: Soon soon soon soon
FIRST: Look at all those pies!
ANYA: HOW UNEXPECTED, HOW SURPRISING!
SECOND: Oowee, oowee
FIRST: That's they way we bake meat pies
SECOND: Ooo-la-la
FIRST: Oh, mein Gott

They laugh. Outside the window is heard gunfire and shouts of "Natasha! Natasha!" Barsukov appears in the doorway.

BARSUKOV: My poor boy!
SEVA: Arrested?
BARSUKOV: They were shooting at Kolya. (*Slumps down in a chair*)

Pirogova faints. The Old Women run out.

SEVA: Where is he?
BARSUKOV: Lying in the corridor.
ANYA: What you can't find in that corridor!

They bring in the wounded Kolya. Enter Yelizaveta Sergeyevna from her room.

YELIZAVETA SERGEYEVNA: You don't know what happened to our cups do you, Kolya? You know, the red ones which are orange. You didn't break them, did you?
NIKOLAI: I don't know.
YELIZAVETA SERGEYEVNA: Lenin gave them to us you know.
NIKOLAI: Sister! Sister of Mercy!

Sister brings him a medicine chest.

SISTER: Bear with it, Nikolai.

SEVA: (*To Dmitry*) What are you standing there for? Do something. You afraid of blood?

DMITRY: No.

SEVA: You'll see worse than this at war. (*Bandages Nikolai*)

BARSUKOV: My poor boy.

YELIZAVETA SERGEYEVNA: What happened this time?

BARSUKOV: Somebody shot him.

PIROGOVA: (*Coming to her senses*) It's Vitya. Only don't beat him up. He's got a bullet in his heart.

SEVA: Yeah, like Kolya does in his foot.

YELIZAVETA SERGEYEVNA: (*Looks out the window*) Vitya! Vitya!

STEPAN IVANOVICH: (*Enters*) So, they've set their sights on us now, too?

PIROGOVA: His father has a bullet in his heart, too.

BARSUKOV: Who, me? (*Looks over his body*)

STEPAN IVANOVICH: What, does it run in the family?

YELIZAVETA SERGEYEVNA: She doesn't mean you, she means the pilot's father.

BARSUKOV: For God's sake.

YELIZAVETA SERGEYEVNA: That Vitya of yours is a strange one. Who does he think he is? You should have a talk with him, Natasha.

PIROGOVA: He's been like that ever since the hospital.

STEPAN IVANOVICH: Concussion, huh?

PIROGOVA: Something like that.

SISTER: When is this war going to end? This is really getting annoying!

ANYA: They say soon.

YELIZAVETA SERGEYEVNA: That's what they always say, and then all they do is turn off the electricity or the water.

SEVA: Well, that does that. (*Finishes putting on the bandage*)

ANYA: Does it hurt?

NIKOLAI: It's nothing. Just a scratch.

PIROGOVA: It's not life-threatening?

STEPAN IVANOVICH: He won't go far now.

BARSUKOV: My poor, poor boy.

SISTER: (*Drinks wine, looks out the window*) These people don't know anything. They sit at work in their ties, walk around under the trees and stroll down the streets in their hats. They don't know anything. It's as if nothing had happened.

ANYA: Not everybody can cry.

SEVA: You mean something has happened already?

PIROGOVA: Look – those women are drinking coffee from cups and the coffee is going up in flames!
YELIZAVETA SERGEYEVNA: What cups are they drinking out of?

The Old Women peer out with the cups and laugh.

FIRST OLD WOMAN: I am a Woman.
SECOND OLD WOMAN: I am a Woman.
FIRST: I am a Woman.
YELIZAVETA SERGEYEVNA: Catch them! Catch them! (*Runs after the Old Women*)
BARSUKOV: Women are inaccesible beings.

The Old Women make an obscene gesture and run away.

PIROGOVA: What's that supposed to mean?
STEPAN IVANOVICH: WOMEN ARE NAKED
UNDER THEIR SHIRTS.
I NEED SOME VODKA,
NEWS LIKE THAT HURTS
YELIZAVETA SERGEYEVNA: (*Returning with the cups*) Here they are. Now let's have some tea.
STEPAN IVANOVICH: So is it tea or vodka?
PIROGOVA: Tea.
SEVA: Or vodka?

They laugh and pour the vodka.

YELIZAVETA SERGEYEVNA: Only just a little bit.

They drink.

ALL: To your health!
To your health!
To your health!
To your health!

YELIZAVETA SERGEYEVNA: Who cut the bread with scissors?
SEVA: Vitya.
ANYA: He glued a naked lady on his airplane!
NIKOLAI: It was him, all right.
PIROGOVA: That's not true! He wouldn't do a thing like that!

A sound is heard. Everyone listens attentively.

YELIZAVETA SERGEYEVNA: You hear that?

Everybody listens attentively again.

BARSUKOV: Think what you will.

ALL: To your health!
     To your health!
     To your health!
     To your health!

ANYA: I'm going to bed.
NIKOLAI: To sleep?
ANYA: I didn't sleep all night long.
SEVA: Sleep is the end!
BARSUKOV: Sleep is death!
STEPAN IVANOVICH: Sleep is health!

ALL: To your health!
     To your health!
     To your health!
     To your health!

PIROGOVA: Alcohol is poison.
DMITRY: Poison is love.
BARSUKOV: Poison is death.
STEPAN IVANOVICH: I've got nothing to say.

ALL: To your health!
     To your health!
     To your health!
     To your health!

BARSUKOV: Hey look! A wolf!
PIROGOVA: Where!
NIKOLAI: Over there.
YELIZAVETA SERGEYEVNA: Where's there a wolf? They scare me to death!
SEVA: (*Looking attentively*) That's no wolf, Yelizaveta Sergeyevna.
PIROGOVA: Who is it then?
STEPAN IVANOVICH: Looks like one to me.
SEVA: (*Looking carefully again*) That's no wolf, Yelizaveta Sergeyevna. It's a bear.
YELIZAVETA SERGEYEVNA: Oh my Lord!
PIROGOVA: Aren't you afraid of them?
ANYA: Wolves, bears – who cares?
NIKOLAI: This is their home, too.
SISTER: Poor animals.
ANYA: (*Looks out the window*) Not one familiar face.
YELIZAVETA SERGEYEVNA: Everything seems to have calmed down out there, now.

They all listen.

BARSUKOV: Just the squirrels gnawing nuts.

They all listen.

PIROGOVA: That's the sound of cherries falling to the ground.

They all listen.

STEPAN IVANOVICH: The same ground the bears stalk.
NIKOLAI: Getting mud on their paws.
YELIZAVETA SERGEYEVNA: Eating raspberries.
SEVA: Scaring off pilots.
DMITRY: There's a whole night ahead of us.
ANYA: As tender as love.

They sit quietly and sing a song.

SCENE SIX

On the Impossible

STEPAN IVANOVICH: Something is happening inside of me and I think
     it's going to burst out! I still believe I can do something for mankind!
     I dreamed about Mendeleev's table of the elements last night. That's
     no coincidence. I'll figure out my mission in this life yet!
YELIZAVETA SERGEYEVNA: I'm so proud of you!
BARSUKOV: It'll pass.
STEPAN IVANOVICH: My whole life I've been on the verge of reaching
     that moment. It's been right there in my grasp. I've been on the brink
     of freedom. And I know my freedom will allow me to do something
     wonderful. It will become something extraordinarily beautiful! I have
     this feeling I'm capable of something and that something is right here
     inside of me!
PIROGOVA: You must be a happy man.
STEPAN IVANOVICH: Must be. What's your name?
PIROGOVA: Natasha.
STEPAN IVANOVICH: "Natasha." What a wonderful name!
YELIZAVETA SERGEYEVNA: Whenever I'm happy I feel like singing.
SEVA: I feel like singing and dancing. Only I only want to do it with
     you – only with you! (*Grabs Sister and they dance*)
BARSUKOV: I've dreamed of playing the trumpet my whole life
     long. All of my feelings remind me of its soaring sound, the joy and

happiness you can hear in it. I want to take a deep breath of air and shout something to the whole world! Confess everything and ask the impossible just once in life!

NIKOLAI: Why don't we abandon this place! Escape! We'll just whip on out of sleeping Moscow and leave it behind doing a hundred and fifty miles an hour on the wet asphalt!

PIROGOVA: Take me with you!

YELIZAVETA SERGEYEVNA: We'll sit on the grass and drink tea!

STEPAN IVANOVICH: Dandelion wine.

BARSUKOV: We'll go fishing and sit by a fire!

ANYA: It will smell of smoke!

NIKOLAI: I'll kiss your rosy cheeks!

ANYA: Behave yourself, you're wounded.

SEVA: Let's go!

They start gathering their things.

SISTER: Maybe let's wait until tomorrow?

All are silent.

STEPAN IVANOVICH: I say we grab a goose by the legs and get the hell out of here!

PIROGOVA: Like in a fairy-tale!

SEVA: Pirogova, your knees are so smooth. My dad always used to say don't marry a girl with bony knees. Wives should have smooth knees.

PIROGOVA: Is that a proposal?

SEVA: No. I say that from the bottom of my heart.

Pirogova crawls under a cabinet and pulls out a kitten.

PIROGOVA: Come live with me, kitty. I'll feed you on fruits.

SEVA: Natasha, can you imagine a kitten that drinks and smokes?

PIROGOVA: I wasn't talking to you.

SEVA: Pity.

PIROGOVA: And you guys were all crying, "Wolf! Wolf!"

Seva opens the window. The sounds of the city and cries of "Natasha! Natasha!" are heard.

PIROGOVA: (*Sticks her head out the window*) Vitya! Vitya!

YELIZAVETA SERGEYEVNA: Natasha, be careful!

PIROGOVA: Vitya! Here I am Vitya!

STEPAN IVANOVICH: Now they'll definitely draw a bead on us.

PIROGOVA: Vitya! I'll be right there! (*Runs out*)

SEVA: Two nuts!

SISTER: He'll kill her!

STEPAN IVANOVICH: What is he shooting out there, a harquebus?

YELIZAVETA SERGEYEVNA: What are you just standing there for? Do something about that thug! Quick!

Seva and Barsukov go out after Pirogova.

STEPAN IVANOVICH: Let him have it!

YELIZAVETA SERGEYEVNA: Only be careful!

ANYA: Bring him back here! I want to get a look at this guy!

The Old Women peer in the window.

FIRST OLD WOMAN: Do you need any cranberries?

SECOND OLD WOMAN: Would you like any cranberries?

They show their basket.

YELIZAVETA SERGEYEVNA: What cranberries? What are you talking about?

FIRST: Go on, have some.

SECOND: It'll only get worse.

They leave.

YELIZAVETA SERGEYEVNA: You mean we haven't suffered through all the tortures yet?

STEPAN IVANOVICH: Are you kidding? This is just the beginning.

YELIZAVETA SERGEYEVNA: My Lord. My Lord.

DMITRY: These days there's even war in Africa.

ANYA: What if the front reaches Moscow?

STEPAN IVANOVICH: The front? Only if it's a cold front.

NIKOLAI: Is that what they say on the radio?

YELIZAVETA SERGEYEVNA: Maybe we ought to have some tea?

SISTER: Isn't there any music on the radio at all?

YELIZAVETA SERGEYEVNA: Let's go out on the veranda and have tea with some of Macintosh's Macintosh apples.

All go out. Dmitry and Sister go further than the rest.

SCENE SEVEN

Dmitry and Sister.

DMITRY: She was wearing a blue dress, she held a flower in her hand,

SISTER: A blue dress of her favorite color.

DMITRY: I looked at her and some man was looking at us.

SISTER: Look out for me! Keep your eyes peeled!

DMITRY: Your eyes look like nothing in the world and I will never forget this for anything in the world!

SISTER: Even if I die?

DMITRY: Death is not for the likes of us.

SISTER: Why?

DMITRY: Alien philosophies are not for us.

SISTER: I have no words in my philosophy.

DMITRY: Because I kiss, kiss, kiss you everywhere!

SISTER: My body is shaking and the earth really is coming out from under my feet!

DMITRY: That's just everything around you shouting – "I want you!"

SISTER: Here?

DMITRY: It's the one time in my life I speak words.

SISTER: You shout them from the Kremlin towers.

DMITRY: It's the changing of the guards!

SISTER: Do you give me your honor?

DMITRY: Forever. For my whole life and this whole minute.

They leave. Andrei watches them go.

ANDREI: I've got nowhere to go at night – this town will love others again. HEY, MOSCOW – I wish I could scream in your face hanging on the step of a train leaving forever. I'll put on my white cape and get in my blue car and I'll drive your streets all night long throwing money at policemen on the way. Just to spite you! I'll ride you up one side and down the other. I'll hit all your romantic parks and all your Crimean Bridges. You'll come begging to me yet!

The sound of a plane flying overhead is heard. Andrei jerks his head up.

That's probably Pirogova flying around up there in the clouds kissing her pilot in weightlessness. Hey, here I am! Right here! (*Laughs*) Only you despise my love. You don't even want to know me. Okay, Moscow. Have it your way. Dance on my grave. (*Leaves. Falls*)

The Old Women, chanting, drag his body off somewhere.

FIRST OLD WOMAN: Dead stop for a dead stop

SECOND OLD WOMAN: Dead body for a dead body

FIRST: Death for the dead

SECOND: Life for the living

FIRST: Black for the black

SECOND: Past for the past

FIRST: Oh, Andrei
SECOND: Oh, my boy
FIRST: All will pass
SECOND: That's all

PART TWO

SCENE ONE

Yelizaveta Sergeyevna, Barsukov and Seva in the room.

BARSUKOV: Here it is morning.
YELIZAVETA SERGEYEVNA: She didn't come home again.
BARSUKOV: What? Yesterday too?
YELIZAVETA SERGEYEVNA: What do you think today is – tomorrow?
BARSUKOV: What's the date today?
YELIZAVETA SERGEYEVNA: I don't understand.
BARSUKOV: Time has lost count.
SEVA: What's the difference? Look, it's light out.
YELIZAVETA SERGEYEVNA: (*Looks out the window*) Headless horsemen keep racing on, racing on on their iron steeds, waving their sabers and shooting off their pistols.
SEVA: I'm going to kill that guy.
YELIZAVETA SERGEYEVNA: Now don't, Seva.
SEVA: Why not? Is he too good for death? I'll squeeze the pistol in both hands, close my eyes and fire!
YELIZAVETA SERGEYEVNA: Call him an ambulance, will you, Barsukov?
BARSUKOV: How about the police?
SEVA: Better off the Red Cross.
YELIZAVETA SERGEYEVNA: Let's give him a shot of some kind.
SEVA: Go on. Put me to sleep. Like a sick dog.
YELIZAVETA SERGEYEVNA: Barsukov, do something with him.

Barsukov tries to do something.

SEVA: Leave me alone! Get your hands off me! Let go of me!
BARSUKOV: Yelizaveta Sergeyevna, help me!
SEVA: Yelizaveta Sergeyevna, do something with me!
BARSUKOV: Help me!
SEVA: No, help me. Help me!

They seat Seva in an easy chair and put a towel to his forehead.

YELIZAVETA SERGEYEVNA: Now, now. Calm down now. You'll grow up soon.

SEVA: I don't know. Somehow that moment never comes.

BARSUKOV: Every time I go to sleep at night I think I'll wake up in the morning a grown-up, too. Only it obviously doesn't work like that.

SEVA: How old are you?

BARSUKOV: Fifty.

SEVA: You're getting up there.

BARSUKOV: Yeah Life's passing me by.

YELIZAVETA SERGEYEVNA: Lately everything seems wrong.

SEVA: But it's still better than nothing. (*Walks around the room collecting flowers*) The whole apartment smells of roses! (*Goes out to throw them out*)

YELIZAVETA SERGEYEVNA: Do you remember how you and I used to go for walks in the Kremlin? It was so clean everywhere. There were flowers and fir-trees and fruit trees on the lawns!

BARSUKOV: And four beehives full of bees for pollination.

YELIZAVETA SERGEYEVNA: Four? There were eight!

They laugh.

BARSUKOV: You remember how you used to come see me? Things were so fine then.

YELIZAVETA SERGEYEVNA: You had something Gypsy-like in your eyes.

BARSUKOV: Everything was so easy and simple. And then it all disappeared. Where did it go?

YELIZAVETA SERGEYEVNA: I don't know.

BARSUKOV: In that little hole by the light of the bats I used to write you batty letters.

YELIZAVETA SERGEYEVNA: You're so nice when you don't drink.

BARSUKOV: I'm nice because I drink.

YELIZAVETA SERGEYEVNA: Only don't go trying to look better than you really are!

BARSUKOV: But I really am much better!

They laugh.

Stepan Ivanovich drinks, too.

YELIZAVETA SERGEYEVNA: You're different.

BARSUKOV: He's the one that's different!

YELIZAVETA SERGEYEVNA: When he drinks he sees God.

They are silent. Enter Pirogova.

PIROGOVA: May I?
BARSUKOV: No. We're naked.
YELIZAVETA SERGEYEVNA: Come in, Natasha.
PIROGOVA: Good morning. You drinking tea?
BARSUKOV: What of it?
YELIZAVETA SERGEYEVNA: Something happen?
PIROGOVA: Naturally.
YELIZAVETA SERGEYEVNA: Seva! Seva!

Enter Seva.

SEVA: Hello, Pirogova. How's things?
PIROGOVA: Andrei drank some trimethyl butane. They took him away in an ambulance!
YELIZAVETA SERGEYEVNA: Oh, my God.
SEVA: Tri-what bu-what?
PIROGOVA: It's some sort of gasoline. But the doctor says his life's not in danger anymore.
SEVA: For Christ's sake! (*Puts on his coat*)
YELIZAVETA SERGEYEVNA: Ask them to give you some medical attention there, while you're at it.
SEVA: I'm all right now.
YELIZAVETA SERGEYEVNA: That's just what worries me.
PIROGOVA: I just saw Dmitry and Sister. They had me worried, too. They said, "Come on, let's go for a tram ride together."
SEVA: So what?
PIROGOVA: So what?! There aren't any trams in Moscow anymore!
YELIZAVETA SERGEYEVNA: What happened to them all?
PIROGOVA: I don't know. I've never seen one, anyway.
BARSUKOV: O-o-kay.
PIROGOVA: What's your whole kitchen splattered in blood for?
YELIZAVETA SERGEYEVNA: Seva slit his wrists yesterday.
PIROGOVA: Seva! Who slits their wrists in a kitchen?!
SEVA: Me. (*Leaves*)
YELIZAVETA SERGEYEVNA: Why not? It's a very cozy kitchen.
PIROGOVA: What's that out your window? Out there in the distance. Is that rye or wheat?
YELIZAVETA SERGEYEVNA: Where?
PIROGOVA: Out there beyond the parachute tower.
BARSUKOV: Let's go take a walk and see.
YELIZAVETA SERGEYEVNA: Maybe you'll have some more tea?
BARSUKOV: No, I'm going. I'm going outside. I'm going to go play soccer with the guys.
PIROGOVA: I'm with you!

They leave. The Old Women peer into the room.

FIRST OLD WOMAN: I feel like eating something.
YELIZAVETA SERGEYEVNA: Have an apple.
FIRST: I already ate a peach.
SECOND: Yesterday I had a banana and I don't want anything more.
FIRST: I feel like eating something.
SECOND: A boy or a girl.
FIRST: A rooster or a rabbit.
SECOND: The rabbit has big, round eyes.
FIRST: Big, round and brown.
SECOND: And sad as they can be.
FIRST: A tear in every one.

Stepan Ivanovich comes out of the neighboring room.

SECOND: (*Sighs*) Oh, mein Gott!
FIRST: All of you, you all of you will be dead.
YELIZAVETA SERGEYEVNA: Begone. We'll live a lot longer than you.

The Old Women laugh. They leave.

STEPAN IVANOVICH: Damn fools!
YELIZAVETA SERGEYEVNA: Ignorant idiots!

SCENE TWO

Yelizaveta Sergeyevna and Stepan Ivanovich stare at each other attentively.

STEPAN IVANOVICH: Some woman is walking around the room smiling.
YELIZAVETA SERGEYEVNA: Some man is looking at me.
STEPAN IVANOVICH: Look at her looking me over.
YELIZAVETA SERGEYEVNA: He's got a radio just like my husband's.
STEPAN IVANOVICH: I take a good look.
YELIZAVETA SERGEYEVNA: I think – it's all over now.
STEPAN IVANOVICH: Wait a minute – that's my wife!
YELIZAVETA SERGEYEVNA: Stepan?
STEPAN IVANOVICH: Liza?
YELIZAVETA SERGEYEVNA: How about that?!
STEPAN IVANOVICH: The wife doesn't recognize her husband, nor the husband his wife.
YELIZAVETA SERGEYEVNA: You haven't seen my glasses, have you?
STEPAN IVANOVICH: No. I don't have my glasses.
YELIZAVETA SERGEYEVNA: Maybe they're in the other room? (*Leaves*)

Stepan Ivanovich pours himself a shot glass. Enter Barsukov.

BARSUKOV: I came back for some reason and can't remember why.

STEPAN IVANOVICH: Maybe you forgot something?

BARSUKOV: I don't remember. Where is Yelizaveta Sergeyevna?

STEPAN IVANOVICH: She lost her glasses. (*Pours a shot glass for Barsukov*)

BARSUKOV: You've got a fine wife. Mine was just the opposite – She always had it in for me. Always digging up evidence against me. A ticket to the attractions at the park or a ticket on that – what do you call it? – river excursion boat. Now I can't remember anything about it. The memory's gone. I don't remember a thing. Except how I used to go fishing when I was a kid. That I remember – every little detail.

STEPAN IVANOVICH: I didn't even know you have a wife.

BARSUKOV: I don't. She died.

STEPAN IVANOVICH: My condolences.

BARSUKOV: Are you kidding! Thank God! What would she think if she saw what is going on these days?! If she were still alive, she'd turn over in her grave!

STEPAN IVANOVICH: May she rest in peace.

They drink. Barsukov looks attentively at Stepan Ivanovich.

BARSUKOV: So it's good she can't see any of this.

STEPAN IVANOVICH: Mine doesn't see anything either.

BARSUKOV: Women are incurable.

STEPAN IVANOVICH: What about you? Do you see anything?!

BARSUKOV: Unfortunately, I do, but …

STEPAN IVANOVICH: I don't see very well either, of course. But at least I listen to the radio every day!

BARSUKOV: You see what I mean?!

STEPAN IVANOVICH: Did you hear – the commun …

Enter Sister. Anya peeks in.

ANYA: Tsss-tsss-tsss-tsss-tsss-tsss-tsss

SISTER: Chh-chh-chh-chh-chh-chh-chh

BARSUKOV: Shh-shh-shh-shh-shh-shh

SISTER: Are you crazy?

ANYA: Mom will hear!

YELIZAVETA SERGEYEVNA: (*Enters*) Have you seen my glasses?

ANYA: We haven't seen anything.

SISTER: Maybe they're in the other room?

YELIZAVETA SERGEYEVNA: Maybe. But they're not there.

BARSUKOV: Maybe you can use mine?

YELIZAVETA SERGEYEVNA: (*Puts on Barsukov's glasses*) Maybe. But I can't see anything with them.

STEPAN IVANOVICH: What is it you want to see? You'd be better off listening to the radio!

YELIZAVETA SERGEYEVNA: Get that nasty thing away from me! This is impossible!

SISTER: Dad!

ANYA: Have you already been drinking this morning?

STEPAN IVANOVICH: Yes!

BARSUKOV: Here we go.

STEPAN IVANOVICH: What do you expect me to do? Live sober? Don't you realize what is going on?!

YELIZAVETA SERGEYEVNA: I don't want to hear about it!

STEPAN IVANOVICH: No, you listen! You listen!

Yelizaveta Sergeyevna goes out. Stepan Ivanovich follows.

YELIZAVETA SERGEYEVNA: Quiet! The children will hear!

STEPAN IVANOVICH: But they don't see a thing!

From the far room we hear the laughter of Yelizaveta Sergeyevna and Stepan Ivanovich.

BARSUKOV: (*Sadly*) Did you hear that?

ANYA: (*Stands on tiptoes*) Only I don't see anything.

SISTER: It was the same thing on Friday.

BARSUKOV: On Friday? I don't remember Friday.

SISTER: (*Laughs*) You don't ever remember anything!

BARSUKOV: Yes. You know, I don't even remember my mother's face when she was young. How I used to go fishing when I was seven – that I remember. I'd catch myself a kilo or two of burbot and bring them home. I remember the burbot, its smell and every single vein. But my mother's young face has not been retained in my memory. I've lost her youthful gaze.

ANYA: You know what I remember? How Andrei braided my hair. He'd get down on his knees and hold the ribbon in his teeth and he would braid my hair with his enormous hands. He'd look me right in the eyes.

SISTER: You were always so small.

ANYA: The past is dead and gone.

BARSUKOV: Did you know that he...

ANYA: Of course I know. But what's age got to do with it? I love his wrinkled face and his strong hands. I never fear anything with him.

SISTER: I would be so happy just to forget it all! Everything that used to be! (*Laughs*) I will always be a lover of absinthe, a lover of cognac, of young boys and their dishevelled little heads. They have different eyes, different bodies. They regret nothing. They have nothing to remember. They have everything you need. Men lead a different life!

Enter Pirogova.

PIROGOVA: Did you completely forget about me? I'm out there waiting for you!
BARSUKOV: Oh, my God, Natasha! I'm sorry!
PIROGOVA: You'll pay for this. You ruined my whole morning!
BARSUKOV: Why don't we go somewhere this evening?
PIROGOVA: No, I can't this evening.
BARSUKOV: On the other hand – you're right. Best not to.
PIROGOVA: Why?
BARSUKOV: I'll fall in love, get married and it'll all start up again.
PIROGOVA: What's that got to do with anything?

They laugh.

If you have something to tell me, tell it to me straight. I never hide a single thought, you know!

Enter Seva and Andrei.

SEVA: Here we are!
PIROGOVA: How are you feeling, Andrei?
BARSUKOV: What's the suitcase for?
ANDREI: I'm leaving today. I've come to say goodbye.
SISTER: You're leaving us?
ANYA: Where are you going?
ANDREI: Home.
PIROGOVA: Is that far?
ANDREI: Very.
ANYA: Shall we have some tea or coffee?
BARSUKOV: Something stronger is in order for an occasion like this. Not everything is trimethyl butane.
ANYA: Trimethyl what?
SEVA: I think that's what they poison mice with.
PIROGOVA: I've got to give you something to remember us by. Will you write to us? You have to write. Your shirt here has a little stain on it – right here on the sleeve – some ink or something. Is there anybody there to take care of you where you're going?

ANDREI: I have a grandmother and sister there.
BARSUKOV: They'll be happy to see you!
SEVA: Well, come on. Let's go.
SISTER: Let's go put the food on the table in the other room!

They leave.

SCENE THREE

The Old Women enter the room.

FIRST OLD WOMAN: You know what? I'm pregnant.
SECOND OLD WOMAN: How long?
FIRST: One day.
SECOND: Then there will be a child.
FIRST: If it's a boy the stomach is round.
SECOND: If it's a girl it is square.
FIRST: What am I going to do?
SECOND: Oh, meine Liebe.
FIRST: Look, here come more guests!

Enter Dmitry.

DMITRY: Hello.
SECOND: Oowee, oowee.
FIRST: Oh, mein Gott!

They laugh and leave. Dmitry sits on a chair. Music and laughter are heard from the other room. Enter Nikolai.

NIKOLAI: Be a friend – lend me some money. Thanks. You really do look like a hero. It's not for nothing they say so. Have you seen Anya?
DMITRY: No. I just got here.
NIKOLAI: She's a sorceress, that girl. Let her out of your sight and she'll slip your grasp. If I could I would follow her upside down on the ceiling! (*He goes into the next room*)

Dmitry sits on a chair. A short while later Yelizaveta Sergeyevna comes in.

YELIZAVETA SERGEYEVNA: Dmitry! What are you sitting here for? Everybody's in there having tea. Today we have mint, rosemary and dog rose petals! (*Leaves*)

We continue to hear music and laughter from the next room. A while later Stepan Ivanovich comes in.

STEPAN IVANOVICH: You see that? They've been dancing all morning long! Have you heard the radio yet today?

DMITRY: No.

STEPAN IVANOVICH: Your loss. By all appearances you're a serious young man. Not like these others. Totally apolitical. Totally! (*Pours drinks for himself and Dmitry. They both drink*)

DMITRY: Thank you.

STEPAN IVANOVICH: You really ought to listen to the radio. Otherwise you go on living and never know a thing. (*Goes out after Yelizaveta Sergeyevna*)

Laughter is still heard from the next room. Enter Seva.

SEVA: Hello, Dmitry. I'm glad you came to see us. There's something I've been wanting to give you. Wait here a second. (*Brings in a huge geographical atlas and gives it to Dmitry*)

DMITRY: Thank you, Seva.

SEVA: There. Take a look at the map of our Homeland.

They turn the pages of the atlas.

The northernmost point is the Fligel Peninsula in the Franz-Josef Land. It lies one thousand kilometers from the North Pole. The southernmost point is further south than Tunis, Gibraltar or the Azores in the Atlantic Ocean. When the sun rises on Ratmanov Island, Moscow is still ushering out the previous day. And when the Kremlin chimes ring midday, it is already evening in Kamchatka.

DMITRY: Great is our Homeland.

SEVA: And look here – the town of Amursk! That almost sounds French. There are even people living way out there.

They are silent.

Aren't you going to say anything? Although, what could you say? What could I possibly hear from you besides those silly words LOVE LOVE LOVE (*Laughs*) What do you care about Moscow? Moscow isn't the center of geography.

DMITRY: I love Moscow.

SEVA: There you go, again! LOVE. Okay, I'll wait until that word loses its meaning, until your lips tire of it, until you can't pronounce it anymore, until it only makes you laugh! LOVE LOVE LOVE – ha-ha-ha – Don't listen to what this town tells you. Don't look in its eyes, or you'll believe what you see there – that's what it's like! Listen to me. I'll tell you the truth. You won't last long here.

DMITRY: Yes I will. But you'd better watch out you don't die laughing.
(*Leaves*)
SEVA: (*Shouts*) When I was twenty I used to beat heroes like that to a pulp!

Yelizaveta Sergeyevna and Stepan Ivanovich peer in the room.

STEPAN IVANOVICH: Well?
SEVA: He left.
YELIZAVETA SERGEYEVNA: (*Gaily*) Did you beat him up?
SEVA: Ah, no big deal. Nailed him a time or two.
YELIZAVETA SERGEYEVNA: (*Ecstatically*) How horrible!
STEPAN IVANOVICH: You did right. It's a family affair.

Yelizaveta Sergeyevna and Seva leave.

How hearts do break. Even without wine. (*Pours a glass and drinks*)

Enter Anya.

ANYA: Papa, explain it to me. Why are we always waiting for some-
thing? When will all the hours and years pass? When does it all end?
When does it come to a conclusion? Why is he leaving? Why is she
always better? Always. No matter what I do. Why?
STEPAN IVANOVICH: Let him leave if he wants to. There's no point in
crying.
ANYA: I always cry when someone leaves.
STEPAN IVANOVICH: It isn't worth it.
ANYA: What else can I do?

Enter Andrei.

STEPAN IVANOVICH: Leaving already? Let's have one for the road.

They pour drinks and down them.

ANYA: Yesterday I was out and around and I bought some new shoes.

All are silent. They look at her shoes.

And then I sat in a café, the one over there across the street. I watched
people going by. It was so strange – not one familiar face.
ANDREI: You were there too early. The jazz band goes on at ten.
Everybody comes to drink and listen to jazz at ten.
ANYA: I was there at seven.
ANDREI: You see what I mean?
ANYA: The waiter there has a bow-tie. And a moustache. Do you
know him?
ANDREI: Yeah.

They are silent.

Well, it's time. (*He embraces Stepan Ivanovich*)
ANYA: I'll see you out.

They leave.

STEPAN IVANOVICH: I've been a bad father all my life. Whenever my children cry I'm ready to do anything for them. Only to this day I don't know what.

> I HOP LIKE A RABBIT
> IN SADNESS AND WOE.
> MAYBE I SHOULD DRINK
> SOME VODKA REAL SLOW?

(*Drinks*) Anya, forgive your foolish father.

Noise and explosions are heard on the street. Everyone comes back in from the next room.

SEVA: You hear that?
NIKOLAI: Again.
YELIZAVETA SERGEYEVNA: A ringing of some sort.
PIROGOVA: Where? Where is it ringing?
STEPAN IVANOVICH: Are they out there blowing something up again?
PIROGOVA: Maybe it's fireworks.
YELIZAVETA SERGEYEVNA: Fireworks? What fireworks? What are you talking about?
SISTER: Maybe something happened?
BARSUKOV: This is great! I like it.

They go out on the street.

SISTER: How beautiful!
NIKOLAI: Seven winds blowing at once!
SEVA: Holy Moses!
PIROGOVA: Maybe today's a holiday?
YELIZAVETA SERGEYEVNA: What holiday? What are you talking about?
NIKOLAI: Have they said anything on the radio, Stepan Ivanovich?
STEPAN IVANOVICH: I'll go give it a listen. (*Leaves*)
SISTER: Look at that red star!
SEVA: It's probably Mars.

The Old Women come out on the street.

FIRST OLD WOMAN: Oowee, oowee.
PIROGOVA: My cat sleeps with open eyes!

SECOND OLD WOMAN: Maybe she's sick?

PIROGOVA: Maybe. She got her tail pinched yesterday.

YELIZAVETA SERGEYEVNA: I don't understand anything. What is going on?

FIRST: White on white.

SECOND: Sunset on sunset.

They all stand there watching what is going on.

SCENE FOUR

Anya and Andrei.

ANYA: What do you see in this city?

ANDREI: I don't know.

ANYA: Do you really think it's so beautiful?

ANDREI: Yes.

ANYA: I don't understand. I just don't understand.

ANDREI: Sometimes even I think I dreamed it up.

ANYA: Maybe I've been looking at it from the wrong angle?

ANDREI: That's not it.

ANYA: Then what is it? Tell me.

ANDREI: You see that boulevard? If you drop an apple here, you'll never catch it again. It'll go rolling down so fast it'll go the whole world 'round.

ANYA: So what?

ANDREI: I can't get a grasp on this town. I can't make contact. It's like the arsonist of Rome – I want my name embellished in this town's history for eternity. I want it to know who I am. I want this place to know I'd do anything for it!

ANYA: Is it really such a big deal?

ANDREI: Not now. Even the stars have grown cold for me in this town.

ANYA: (*Laughs*) Take me with you! Let's get out of here! The sooner the better! Let's go! We'll sail above the red brick walls, skimming over all the towers and all the poplars and then we'll be far, far away! You'll be better off there, you'll never shed a single tear! OPEN YOUR EYES! OPEN YOUR EYES!

ANDREI: All my dreams are slipping away! (*Laughs*) There it goes – the life I was never even able to taste. It broke me! OPEN YOUR EYES! OPEN YOUR EYES!

ANYA: Happiness is waiting for us where Moscow's boulevards come to an end!

They are carried off by the wind and we don't see them anymore. All we see are the roofs of the houses and the tops of swings peering through the trees. The Old Women, looking up, watch them go. Nikolai sits on a balcony and watches everything from above.

FIRST OLD WOMAN: Take a look at those angels, why don't you!
SECOND OLD WOMAN: That's enough of your insolence!
FIRST: What's the day today?
SECOND: Today is Tuesday.
FIRST: What's the date today?
SECOND: Today is the seventh.
FIRST: What time is it?
NIKOLAI: (*Looks at his watch*) Nine.
SECOND: Poppycock!
FIRST: (*Sighs*) Oh, Liebe meine.

They leave. Enter Seva.

SEVA: What are you moping around here about?
NIKOLAI: Love.
SEVA: Nonsense. Give your friend a call and have her snuffed out.
NIKOLAI: What?!
SEVA: You got other thoughts on the subject?
NIKOLAI: Yes. I'm going to the front.
SEVA: They'll kill you.
NIKOLAI: I'm better off dying for my country than having it happen here for no good reason.
SEVA: Don't be silly. You can die from love anywhere you want. Although you'll look good in a military uniform. And you'll learn to shoot.
NIKOLAI: I already know how. (*Pulls out a pistol and shoots*)
SEVA: (*Looks over the pistol*) For a soldier even a song is a weapon.
NIKOLAI: Aren't you ashamed to be sitting it out in Moscow?
SEVA: I've already done my time. Want a drink?
NIKOLAI: No.
SEVA: Then I'll finish it. Take a lesson from me – I do everything all the way. I smoke cigarettes down to the filter and I watch films to the end even when they're sad and I don't like them.
NIKOLAI: I don't smoke.
SEVA: Then have a cigarette and let's go. I'll show you some real women. Want to?
NIKOLAI: Yeah. I do.
SEVA: Great! We'll go see Lucy!

NIKOLAI: Who's that?
SEVA: LUCY?

Barsukov walks down the street with his arms around the two Old Women.

BARSUKOV: What? You mean you don't know her yet?

The Old Women howl with laughter.

SEVA: She lives on the sunny side of a cherry tree branch.
BARSUKOV: Number eight, Cozy Street.
SEVA: She has a golden heart.
BARSUKOV: And golden hands!
SEVA: And a gold tooth.
BARSUKOV: She makes great coffee!
SEVA: She's not married.
BARSUKOV: She leads a hedonistic life.
SEVA: But she looks great.
BARSUKOV: She used to sing in the opera!
SEVA: She's a sophisticate in music.
BARSUKOV: She's all in silk. Every inch!
NIKOLAI: Let's go.
BARSUKOV: Hurrah! It's off to Lucy we shall go

They laugh.

NIKOLAI: Lucy – I think she's a goddess! She laughs when she makes
    Arabian coffee and diamonds sparkle on her fingers!
SEVA: You can forget everything when you're in her hands!
NIKOLAI: Let's go knock on her door!
BARSUKOV: Let's go quick!
NIKOLAI: Let's go get burned!

Seva and Nikolai leave. The Old Women won't let Barsukov go.

FIRST: Don't go!
SECOND: You promised!

Yelizaveta Sergeyevna comes out of the house.

BARSUKOV: Liza! Liza!
YELIZAVETA SERGEYEVNA: What?
FIRST: Don't think badly of him
SECOND: He always drinks like a gentleman
FIRST: It's not as if he's not in a holiday mood when he drinks
SECOND: He only drinks on holidays
FIRST: But look how many holidays there are!

SECOND: Just a couple here and there
FIRST: But always a gentleman
SECOND: And he recites poetry
FIRST: You wouldn't believe it!
YELIZAVETA SERGEYEVNA: You're drunk again.
BARSUKOV: I can be drunk for walking the streets. I can be drunk for making love. But I can't be drunk for making art!
FIRST: Fet![2]
SECOND: A real Fet!

They clap their hands.

YELIZAVETA SERGEYEVNA: Let's go home. You need to get some sleep.
BARSUKOV: What for? And cross another day out of my life? No way!
FIRST: Let's go!
SECOND: Let's go!
FIRST: You promised!
BARSUKOV: Liza! Liza!
YELIZAVETA SERGEYEVNA: Oh, mein Gott! (*She leads Barsukov out*)

SCENE FIVE

Dmitry's room. Dmitry and Sister.

DMITRY: You and I are racing head-on into catastrophe. We've forgotten the rules, the brakes, the stop signals, the street signs, and all the other red circles and triangles that run along your body. Right in the middle of the highway all the wires got tangled up in the sheets. Trolleys ride the ceiling and thunder through the tunnels. Subway trains are shaking our room.
SISTER: At this dark time of day the store signs make your face
MULTI-COLORED
DMITRY: They change the world
SISTER: Make fun of my eyes
DMITRY: Turn your face into someone else's
SISTER: Break reality into layers

---

[2] Afanasy Fet was one of the best Russian poets of the 19th century. The Old Women are being ironic. Barsukov is not quoting poetry. Because Fet's name is unlikely to be recognized by an English-speaking audience, the Old Women's lines might be replaced in performance with "A poet!" and "A real poet!"

DMITRY: Bind us in one single knot
SISTER: Tighter and tighter
DMITRY: For all life long!

The door opens. Someone's steps are heard.

SISTER: You hear that?
DMITRY: Your heart is beating beneath my shoulder-blade.

Enter Seva.

SEVA: Are you sleeping? No? I was just walking by and I thought to myself, I thought, why don't I stop in for a little visit? Go ahead and sleep. Sleep. (*Sits on a chair*) I'm like a beast in autumn today – I keep wandering through the woods, looking under the fir branches. I want to eat someone, drink some blood, rip someone to shreds. Or no. (*To Sister*) Drag you into my lair, embrace you and fall asleep for the whole winter. I want to get snowed in, covered over with snow-drifts. I want to skip over December, January and February until all the snow melts, until some love-crazy pilot comes along shooting off his gun.
DMITRY: You want something to drink?
SEVA: Easy now. You think I came looking for a fight?
DMITRY: I don't know.
SEVA: You're right. I came here to kill you.

They are silent.

I bought a Colt from Kolya. Like it? (*Puts the pistol on the table*)
DMITRY: No.

They are silent as they look at the pistol.

SEVA: I do. Well? How come you aren't asking any questions? Huh?
DMITRY: I did.
SEVA: Wrong question.
DMITRY: Why?
SEVA: You ask – I'll answer.
DMITRY: I asked.
SEVA: How come you aren't asking any questions? Ask me something! I mean, you don't know anything about me! I'm a wild-man. I'm a lunatic.
SISTER: Now listen here …
SEVA: I've got the perfect alibi. At this very moment I'm not here, I'm at number eight Cozy Street. And I've got witnesses. How do you like that?
DMITRY: You're smart.

SEVA: That's very bad. Very bad.
SISTER: All right. You've been with that … that … that … woman?!
SEVA: (*Laughs*) Yes!
SISTER: You promised!

Seva laughs.

   I'll strangle you!
SEVA: Strangle me!
SISTER: You… (*Throws everything she can get her hands on at Seva. He laughs and fends off the flying objects*)
SEVA: You'd strangle me easier!

Sister grabs the pistol. Dmitry and Seva race at her. They struggle, shout, grab at each others' arms, hit each other and choke each other.

   What a day! Everybody is out to strangle me!

They race around the room, knocking over the furniture and shouting,
"YOU YOU YOU YOU BOOM BOOM BOOM BOOM."
"BANG BANG BANG BANG BANG BANG BANG BANG."
Seva shoots at Dmitry. Dmitry shoots at Seva.

SISTER: That thing's no toy!
SEVA: I missed! I missed!
SISTER: You wounded him.
DMITRY: I hit him?
SEVA: You hit me.

Sister gets out a medicine box and bandages Seva.

SISTER: You…
SEVA: You…
DMITRY: You…
SISTER: You idiot idiot idiot
DMITRY: I'm sorry.
SISTER: Only don't die. Don't die. (*Cries*)
SEVA: (*Wipes her tears*) Crocodile tears.
SISTER: You monkey.

They embrace and weep. Dmitry laughs.

SISTER: Knock that off right now. This is no time for hysterics.
DMITRY: Oh is that so?!
SISTER: That's right!
DMITRY: What is going on here?
SISTER: It's a nightmare.

SEVA: Life is very strange.
DMITRY: It's beyond me.
SISTER: Shut up.

They are silent.

DMITRY: Here's my life – take it! Take it if you have no heart, if you never weep. Take it! Drink my young blood! I'm twenty years old and I DON'T LOVE YOU! I wouldn't say anything more about myself even if you begged me! So there! You have no heart! You only live through me! Go ahead and try it now without me! You and all your schemes! I'm air! I'm out of here! (*Runs out, slams the door. He knocks over an Old Woman*)
FIRST OLD WOMAN: Hey!
SECOND OLD WOMAN: Ho!
FIRST: O-ho-ho-ho
SECOND: Oa-ha-ha-ha
FIRST: Ah-yai-yai-yai
SECOND: Oh-oh-oh-oh

Sister rubs iodine on the Old Woman's scratch.

SISTER: Quick as a jiffy.
FIRST: And just as iffy.
SECOND: Will she live to the wedding?
SEVA: I don't think she'll make it.
FIRST: Oh, mein Gott!
SECOND: Oh, meine Liebe!

Sister leads out the wounded Seva. Seva supports the wounded Old Woman. Doors slam throughout the house. Cars and trucks are still humming out on the street and street lamps are swaying. Only there's nobody here to see it. ALL HAVE LEFT.

SCENE SIX

Yelizaveta Sergeyevna, Stepan Ivanovich, Pirogova and Barsukov in the house.

PIROGOVA: Look! Look! It's snowing!
BARSUKOV: Oh yeah.
STEPAN IVANOVICH: Now we'll have another three months of cold.
BARSUKOV: Yeah, the cold is intolerable. So is the heat.
YELIZAVETA SERGEYEVNA: It will be New Years soon!

BARSUKOV: One time we planned to greet the New Year in a restaurant. We waited and waited. The whole restaurant waited. But it came an hour late!

PIROGOVA: You think that's something? I once heard how one family planned to greet the New Year. They cooked a duck, put a spread on the table and popped the corks on the champagne. And they waited and waited, and it never did come!

STEPAN IVANOVICH: Maybe they just did a bad job of seeing the old year out?

BARSUKOV: Probably.

PIROGOVA: You think it will come to us?

STEPAN IVANOVICH: I think at least it'll stop in for a peek.

BARSUKOV: Granted, it's not as if this is a whole city here.

YELIZAVETA SERGEYEVNA: Every home is its own private Moscow.

PIROGOVA: I love New Years!

YELIZAVETA SERGEYEVNA: Kids love it when every year brings something new. For old people every one takes something away.

PIROGOVA: I keep thinking, what if it doesn't come?

YELIZAVETA SERGEYEVNA: It will. It definitely will come.

BARSUKOV: It's got nowhere else to go.

STEPAN IVANOVICH:

> A PRICKLY CHRISTMAS TREE
> GROWS CALMLY ON THE LEE.
> NOW THERE'S A REASON STRAIGHT AND TRUE
> TO HAVE MYSELF A DRINK OR TWO.

They pour and drink.

YELIZAVETA SERGEYEVNA: Listen. Footsteps.

Steps are heard.

PIROGOVA: Isn't today a little early?

BARSUKOV: You never can tell.

STEPAN IVANOVICH: Anything can happen.

YELIZAVETA SERGEYEVNA: Maybe someone's come to visit?

Enter Seva and Sister.

Oh, look who's here!

SEVA: Here we are!

BARSUKOV: We were all ready to usher in the New Year.

SEVA: What? Without us?

PIROGOVA: You gave us a good scare!

YELIZAVETA SERGEYEVNA: Sit down here at the table! Today we've got tea and milk!

SEVA: Sounds great!

PIROGOVA: What happened to your hand?

SEVA: A brigand's bullet.

YELIZAVETA SERGEYEVNA: Bullets again? They're shooting again?

STEPAN IVANOVICH: The pilot?

SEVA: No. Just a stray.

YELIZAVETA SERGEYEVNA: Isn't that something? Does it hurt?

SEVA: No, no. It's okay.

STEPAN IVANOVICH: Fine thing to call okay.

SEVA: Hey Pirogova, when are you going to introduce us to the pilot?

BARSUKOV: I haven't heard anything of him for ages.

YELIZAVETA SERGEYEVNA: Thank God!

PIROGOVA: It turns out he's got a wife.

YELIZAVETA SERGEYEVNA: What?

PIROGOVA: And eight kids.

YELIZAVETA SERGEYEVNA: You're kidding!

PIROGOVA: But it's not his fault.

STEPAN IVANOVICH: Poor girl.

PIROGOVA: His wife is a really great cook. (*Wipes her tears*)

BARSUKOV: That's bad.

PIROGOVA: Maybe I should write him a letter?

YELIZAVETA SERGEYEVNA: Letters are no good. They don't understand letters.

BARSUKOV: There you have it.

YELIZAVETA SERGEYEVNA: Why don't we have some tea.

SISTER: Tea or coffee?

PIROGOVA: Tea.

BARSUKOV: Or coffee?

They laugh and move the cups about.

YELIZAVETA SERGEYEVNA: We used to ride up to the Sokol neighborhood for milk. We'd get on the bus, each of us with a milk-can. We'd ride way up on the hill, looking out from side to side. The houses in Sokol are beautiful and the trees are big. We'd just look at them out the windows. We'd get there, buy our milk and come home again. Sokol has changed, of course. And anyway you can buy milk anywhere now. It used to be you could only get it in Sokol. That was the only place.

BARSUKOV: The blackberries up in Sokol were good, too. You'd scratch your hands all up before plucking any off the vine.

YELIZAVETA SERGEYEVNA: So you used to go pinching from other people's gardens, did you?

BARSUKOV: That was a long time ago. You probably don't even remember it.

YELIZAVETA SERGEYEVNA: My dear man! I still remember when there were nothing but horses on the Arbat. Not a car in sight!

They laugh.

SISTER: Natasha, don't cry!

SEVA: You want me to put some music on?

PIROGOVA: What music?

SEVA: Real Moscow music.

STEPAN IVANOVICH: What's to cry about? Come on, let's dance.

PIROGOVA: You see out there, way off in the distance, that little grave in the middle of the wheat stacks? See that little mound there? Over there! Over there! That's where I buried my kitten. She abandoned me, too.

YELIZAVETA SERGEYEVNA: Poor thing.

PIROGOVA: Now she'll get covered with snow.

STEPAN IVANOVICH: Have a shot of vodka, sweetheart.

Pirogova drinks.

SISTER: Now how do you feel?

PIROGOVA: Bad.

SISTER: (*Doesn't hear*) Thank God.

YELIZAVETA SERGEYEVNA: (*Laughs*) What are you so mean about?

SISTER: I'll be good tomorrow. And I'll have a different dress.

STEPAN IVANOVICH: Are you crying, too?

SISTER: No. I'm laughing.

STEPAN IVANOVICH: I love it when you laugh.

All laugh, drink tea and dance.

YELIZAVETA SERGEYEVNA: Seva, turn the music up louder! Louder! Louder!

STEPAN IVANOVICH: We'll still make mankind happy yet!

BARSUKOV: Why don't I play something on the trumpet? (*Plays the trumpet*)

SCENE SEVEN

Dmitry stands by the house. He holds a pistol in his hand and looks in the window.

DMITRY: God is my witness. I held off as long as I could. (*Loads the pistol*)

Nikolai passes by in a military uniform with a backpack on his back.

NIKOLAI: You out for a walk? You look horrible. Come on, out with it. What happened?

DMITRY: I've got nothing more to say.

NIKOLAI: I'm going off to war.

DMITRY: When?

NIKOLAI: Right now. Two days on the train and I'll be there. My dream came true.

DMITRY: You come to say goodbye?

NIKOLAI: No. I'll write my dad later from the front. I wouldn't be able to take it right now. So I guess I'll be a scoundrel. Maybe I'll get killed in the war for that.

DMITRY: You won't get killed.

NIKOLAI: Why do you think that?

DMITRY: I don't know.

NIKOLAI: Here – have a smoke.

They light up. The smoke floats in big clouds for a long time.

DMITRY: You know, I didn't want to tell anybody, but I'm going away, too.

NIKOLAI: When are you going?

DMITRY: I'm going right now, too. I've even got my weapon with me. (*Shows his pistol*)

NIKOLAI: I had one just like that.

DMITRY: I know how to parachute.

NIKOLAI: That doesn't scare you?

DMITRY: No.

NIKOLAI: They're dancing.

DMITRY: Mankind has danced since time immemorial.

NIKOLAI: Everything in Moscow has changed.

DMITRY: Yeah, but there are still girls out there in the streets. With their scarfs fluttering up over their left shoulders.

NIKOLAI and DMITRY: (*Shouting*) HEY GIRLS! OVER HERE! HERE WE COME! WE'RE COMING TO KISS YOU!

They laugh and leave, singing a song. The two Old Women wave goodbye with their handkerchiefs.

FIRST OLD WOMAN: They look like heroes.

SECOND OLD WOMAN: I don't know.

FIRST: That's what everybody says.

END OF PLAY

Other titles in the Russian Theatre Archive series:

This book is part of a series. The publisher will accept continuation orders which may be cancelled at any time and which provide for automatic billing and shipping of each title in the series upon publication. Please write for details.